Quarterly Essay

CONTENTS

Quarterly Essay is published four times a year by Black Inc., an imprint of Schwartz Publishing Pty Ltd
Publisher: Morry Schwartz

ISBN 186-395-1822
ISSN 1832-0953

Subscriptions (4 issues): $49 a year within Australia incl. GST (Institutional subs. $59). Outside Australia $79. Payment may be made by Mastercard, Visa or Bankcard, or by cheque made out to Schwartz Publishing. Payment includes postage and handling.

To subscribe, fill out and post the subscription card, or subscribe online at:

www.quarterlyessay.com

Correspondence and subscriptions should be addressed to the Editor at:

Black Inc.
Level 5, 289 Flinders Lane
Melbourne VIC 3000 Australia
Phone: 61 3 9654 2000
Fax: 61 3 9654 2290
Email:
quarterlyessay@blackincbooks.com (editorial)
subscribe@blackincbooks.com (subscriptions)

Editor: Chris Feik
Management: Sophy Williams
Production Co-ordinator: Caitlin Yates
Publicity: Anna Lensky
Design: Guy Mirabella

WHAT'S LEFT? | The Death of Social Democracy

Clive Hamilton

LABOR LOST

In May 2002, at the invitation of Senator Kim Carr, I addressed the national conference of the ALP/Trade Union Left, which is held annually in Canberra. In thinking about what I would say, I tossed up whether to play it safe and state the usual things about social injustice and the Howard government's penchant for penalising the most vulnerable, or to take a risk and give voice to my growing sense of the irrelevance of the traditional Left arising from its failure to develop a politics that resonated with the times. This was the view I was to publish a year later in my book *Growth Fetish*, but in 2002 I was still reluctant to criticise those on the progressive side of politics whose commitment to social justice remained undimmed while all those around them, including the dominant faction in the Labor Party, had been seduced by the neo-liberal story of the wonders of the free market.

Deciding that for its own good the Left needed to be challenged rather than massaged, I addressed the hundred or so delegates without pulling any punches. I argued that they, and the Left more generally, were bereft of ideas, that they were wandering in the wilderness mouthing the same old slogans to people who no longer wanted to hear them. In the face of a market fundamentalism that carried all before it, the Left had failed to understand that the world had been transformed in ways that rendered their ideas impotent and irrelevant.

"We must face up to the facts," I lectured. "While rooted in historical reality, the Left's 'deprivation model', which insists that the mass of people are suffering from material deprivation, is today the opposite of the truth. The dominant characteristic of contemporary Australia is not deprivation but abundance."

I went on to talk about income levels scarcely imaginable in the 1950s, about the love of consumer goods, the soaring demand for private schooling and the comfortable suburbs filled to bursting with DVDs, swimming pools and 4WDs. I also talked about money hunger, overwork, perceived meaninglessness and the sicknesses of affluence, and pointed to the great contradiction of modern politics:

> Despite the fantastic promises of material progress, and the extraordinary success of capitalism in delivering undreamt-of wealth for ordinary people, we have to make a horrible admission — the people are still not happy.

I finished off by calling for a politics based on a new understanding of a society characterised by both widespread prosperity and entrenched alienation, a politics that would help people to step out of the gilded cage and experience true autonomy and authentic lives, a politics for a society in which citizens are committed to "a rich life rather than a life of riches".

Not unexpectedly, the speech elicited strong reactions, both immediately and in the weeks following. As I sat down — catching a glimpse of a shell-shocked Kim Carr, who later let on that it would never again fall to him to invite the conference's guest speaker — some on the more traditional, trade-union wing of the Left stood to condemn me for abandoning the poor, for failing to understand the extent of material deprivation in underprivileged areas, and for ignoring the problems caused by growing inequality. Voices of support, by contrast, were muted.

But as the session broke up and delegates spilled out of the room, it became apparent that others had found my "provocation", as one termed it, a breath of fresh air. They too had been wondering if the old-left view of the world had been out-run by history. Among the many comments that I received – including reactions to a newspaper opinion piece a few days later summarising the argument – were the following:

> Congratulations ... Your emphasis on the consumer society, affluence, etc., is extremely timely.

> Let me remind you of some salient facts you have omitted in your portrayal of contemporary Australia as "enormously wealthy" ...

> Your article was the most refreshing thing I have read in a newspaper for a long time and gives me confidence that the issues you raised are on the agenda.

> After reading extracts in the press of your rather shallow recent speech I am inclined to think that people like you tend to live in your own little insulated world and assume that everyone else shares the same inflated salary etc. that you enjoy.

> I was present when Clive Hamilton spoke. He has a valid point, albeit delivered in a rather over-the-top way.

> While your paper may have been confronting to some, I think it was generally well received. It was certainly a key topic of conversation at lunch and most who I spoke to were very positive.

The events of the conference were reported by the journalist Glenn Milne in his Monday column in the *Australian*, where he suggested that the demand for a new direction "went over like a lead balloon". One who was not at the conference, because he was part of the ALP's Right faction, reacted with characteristic gusto. The "shadow assistant treasurer" Mark Latham wrote in an email discussion group:

> This is the ultimate sell-out of the Green Left: post-material basket-weaving for gentrified inner-city types like Clive, while those of us in the suburbs should simply forget about the public housing estates down the road, with their 40 per cent unemployment rates and 80 per cent welfare dependency. "Let them eat lentils" seems to be the Hamilton mantra. How pathetic.

Latham, whom I had unkindly referred to in my speech as the Sage of Werriwa, followed up with an opinion piece along the same lines in the Murdoch broadsheet a fortnight later. Yet, as we will see, by the time he became leader of the Labor Party four years later, Mark Latham seemed to have undergone something of a transformation. This essay is an attempt to track the wider meaning of that transformation, and to take up the unfinished business it represents for the ALP and the nation.

In the latter part of the nineteenth century, the emerging labour parties found their political identity: they were social democratic parties, some of whose members, especially those in the trade unions, went further and gave their allegiance to democratic socialism. The distinction between social democracy and democratic socialism was always blurred, but it roughly reflected a difference over the extent to which the means of production should be publicly owned. In practice, though, the side one took reflected not so much a judgment about how best to manage the economy for the benefit of working people, but the degree of anti-capitalist sentiment that animated the party member.

Social democracy has always supported private ownership of the means of production, as opposed to extensive public ownership, although for most of its history it advocated "a mixed economy" with public owner-ship of strategic sectors of the economy. These sectors sometimes included industries subject to natural monopoly (telecommunications, ports) and of national economic importance.

By contrast, democratic socialists were more likely to argue that gov-ernment should assert greater control over the economy and that this required state ownership of the "commanding heights", especially the banks, whose investment decisions were so crucial to economic per-formance and thus to the welfare of the working class.

The division marked the Australian Labor Party throughout much of its history. Over time, however, the number of peaks in the commanding heights picked out by Labor dwindled. While in 1947 Ben Chifley attempted to nationalise the banks, by 1991 attitudes had shifted so sharply that Paul Keating could boast of his success in selling off the Commonwealth Bank, the "people's bank".

The original socialist aspiration of the Australian Labor Party remains enshrined in its constitution today. Its first objective is set out as follows:

> The Australian Labor Party is a democratic socialist party and has
> the objective of the democratic socialisation of industry, produc-
> tion, distribution and exchange, to the extent necessary to eliminate
> exploitation and other anti-social features in these fields.

That this declaration is an historical anachronism rather than an active principle is confirmed by the fact that it was for the most part Labor gov-ernments, federal and state, that carried out the wave of privatisations of "socialised" industries in the 1980s. The so-called Blackburn gloss added to the socialist objective in 1921 – the words "to the extent necessary to eliminate exploitation" – provided a rationale for the sell-offs. Not that one was needed, for by the mid-1980s no one was arguing for public ownership of industry. Using the weapon of "the public interest", the Left of the Labor Party fought a rear-guard action against the privatisations, but its indignation was based more on a reluctance to cave in to the demands of market fundamentalism than on cogent argument. And its indignation was not sufficient to cause it to jeopardise party unity.*

In managing the economy, both social democrats and democratic socialists aimed to smooth the cycles of an inherently unstable system held hostage by the "animal spirits" of the wealthy, who periodically frightened social democratic governments with threats of a capital strike, that is, moving investment offshore. Labor's goal was to ensure that the living conditions of working people were the first priority of government, and that maintaining employment always took precedence over controlling inflation. After the Second World War, the ideas of J.M. Keynes ruled economic policy, and they provided the theory to sustain these commitments.

From its earliest days, social democracy was animated by a single emotion, outrage at material deprivation and exploitation of working people and corresponding anger at the privilege of those who profit from the capitalist economic system. Perhaps the sense of grievance at the unfairness of the system is best captured in a wry piece of Latin American graffito: "If shit turned to gold, the poor would be born without arses." This sentiment motivated the core demand for social justice, which included greater equality in the distribution of resources and the creation of a welfare system that would protect the populace when capitalism failed to provide a decent standard of living. Progressive income tax systems and the welfare state are the great legacies of social democracy.

---

* This is not to say that there were not some compelling arguments against at least some of the privatisations carried out by the Hawke-Keating governments and some state counterparts. The sale of the Commonwealth Serum Laboratories (CSL) in 1994 was an especially bad decision made for purely ideological reasons with no regard to the financial interests of the owners of the asset – the Australian public. The sale was pushed through without any analysis of the financial implications by the finance minister of the day, Kim Beazley. According to an analysis based on conservative assumptions, it has been estimated that the Australian public will over time be worse off by $600 million as a result of the sale. It is likely that proper financial analysis would also have ruled out sales of airports and Telstra but may have favoured the privatisation of Qantas and the Commonwealth Bank – although fifteen years down the track the long-suffering customers of the people's bank are still wondering when the efficiency dividend will materialise.

Beneath the political demands lay a social analysis in which the central concept was power. The striking characteristic of early social democratic theory was the recognition, owed in large measure to Karl Marx, that the concentration of control over capital in the hands of a few led to unequal power relations. This recognition gave rise to a natural alliance between social democrats and trade unionists. As the bosses exercised power in the workplace and in the wider political sphere, the Left organised to counter it in both of these arenas.

As it turned out, social democracy and trade unionism saved capitalism from self-destruction, both by ensuring that the fruits of increased productivity were more fairly distributed than they would otherwise have been, and by protecting the working class from the worst effects of economic downturns. While employers and their conservative political barrackers have for decades fulminated against the "irresponsible and unaffordable" demands of trade unions on behalf of their members, constantly rising real wages for the traditional working class were the price of social harmony and served as an ever-present spur to further productivity gains. Regular wage rises might have been painful for individual employers, but they were essential to the flourishing of the system. It is the argument of this essay that sustained increases in living standards for the great bulk of working people have so transformed social conditions as to render social democracy redundant as a political ideology.

In the early 1970s, a crisis in the world economy caused a tectonic shift in the realm of politics. In short, social democracy was mugged by stagflation. In the past, social democratic governments had sought to control inflation by damping the economy through tightening the money supply. Now a combination of high unemployment and high inflation – "stagflation" – made that course of action politically impossible. Lengthening already-long dole queues was unacceptable to social democrats, yet it was not clear how inflation could be tamed otherwise. President Nixon's decision in 1972 to abandon the global system of fixed exchange rates known as Bretton Woods unleashed a new era of international economic unpredictability, especially when combined with the effects of the doubling of oil prices in 1973. In the process social democrats found it increasingly difficult simultaneously to protect the vulnerable and appear to be credible economic managers.

In Australia, the Whitlam government was a spectacular casualty of the new dispensation. Whitlam's prediction on the steps of Parliament House on 11 November 1975 that nothing would save the Governor-General proved incorrect: the Dismissal was not just the end of a government that had dreams grander than "responsible economic management", it also marked the beginning of the end of the era of social democracy. The ghost of the Whitlam government has stalked the Labor Party ever since, turning visionary social reformers into cautious economic managers desperate to prove that they can be trusted to put their hands on the economic levers.

The end of Keynesian economic management robbed social democracy of its most powerful weapon. Keynes' endorsement of interventionist fiscal policy, and his scepticism about the wisdom of leaving the fate of millions to the whims of self-interested investors, was understood to be the natural approach of social democracy. Global capital mobility rendered this view hard to defend and Labor leaders felt compelled to attend assiduously to the sensitivities of the big end of town in a way never before contemplated.

The advent of stagflation also made possible the ascendancy of the political philosophy now known as neo-liberalism. In the early days neo-liberalism rode on the back of monetarism, the belief that inflation, and macroeconomic performance more generally, depends on the money supply alone and that governments through their central banks should put price stability before all else. Milton Friedman and the other monetarists were fervent, at times fanatical, advocates of the free market and minimal government. By the 1980s their argument that inflation must be tackled first to protect the value of assets had won the day. Inflation was the dragon that ate social democracy and, thus nourished, gave birth to neo-liberalism. Social justice found itself up against new enemies – fiscal conservatism and tight money. It took a decade before, on one day in 1983, the battle for the heart of the Labor Party was finally won by these foes.

Great historical shifts are often implemented by a handful of men who do not comprehend the larger forces that guide them. When the Hawke government was first elected in 1983, the new treasurer, Paul Keating, was an economic innocent. The Labor Party had wrestled with economic and social policy for years in opposition, and by the time of the election it had a well-developed social democratic platform designed to strengthen Australian industry and promote the growth of high-quality jobs. The platform was put to the country and was popular enough, at a time of high unemployment and high inflation, to help Labor win power. As shadow minister for minerals and energy during the period when the platform was being prepared, Keating played no part in its formulation.

Among the new Treasurer's staff was economist John Langmore, who had transferred from shadow treasurer Ralph Willis's office. A self-described Christian socialist, Langmore had played a central role in developing the economic platform. But the new Treasurer was also being advised by his department, then dominated by its secretary, John Stone. Immediately after the election Stone presented Hawke and Keating with a memorandum arguing that there was only one immediate priority for macroeconomic policy: to reduce government spending. He claimed to show that the previous treasurer, John Howard, had misled the country about the extent of the growth in public spending during Fraser's last year in power, and that without severe restraint there would be a major blow-out in the deficit with dire consequences for the economy.

Stone was a powerful figure in Canberra, an economist whose influence was pervasive enough for the era to be dubbed by some the Stone Age. By predisposition he was right-wing, but his Keynesian training still exerted a vestigial influence. He was in transition to the most radical free-market position, and for a time even opposed the floating of the Australian dollar.

Keating was ideologically inclined towards the Treasury line, although he gave no clue of this during the 1983 election campaign. A few days after Labor's victory, Stone invited the Treasurer over for a chat — "no need to bring your staff," he said. Later that week, Keating said that he was going to do exactly what Treasury advised him, because that was where the intellectual strength was and that was the way he had learnt to survive while a minister in the Whitlam government. He had been a minister then for only a few weeks, but they were enough for him to observe at close hand how the economy had destroyed the last Labor government. The visionary Treasurer had now found his vision and if that meant jettisoning decades of Labor tradition, so be it. Those of his staff, like Langmore, who remained loyal to the social democratic idea, were soon replaced by advocates of the free market, and so began the process whereby Labor became just as comfortable outflanking the Coalition from the right as from the left.

On that day in 1983, the fate of social democracy in Australia was sealed. The words of John Stone were so convincing that Paul Keating was in 1984 named Finance Minister of the Year by the money market magazine *Euromoney*. Ironically, the world's greatest treasurer proved so successful at using tight money to suppress inflation at the expense of employment that the ALP is even today attacked by the Coalition for presiding over interest rates of 18 per cent in 1985. (After the fall of the Keating government in 1996, a senior Treasury official bragged on *Four Corners* that Treasury got up more of its neo-liberal economic agenda under Labor than it ever could have under a conservative government.)

Although the left-wing of the ALP opposed much of the economic rationalist agenda implemented by Labor over the next thirteen years, it was unable to develop a coherent alternative. Nor was it willing to threaten party unity when all seemed to be going so well electorally. Yet the social consequences were far-reaching. In 1998, two years after Keating's demise, the revolt against "economic rationalism" and globalisation burst through not from the left but from the right, in the form of

Hansonism. It brought with it some very unpleasant side-effects, notably attacks on Aboriginal welfare, Asian immigration and gun-control laws. Much of the disquiet that had festered since the early 1980s – when the Labor Party began its thirteen years of uninterrupted rule – became focused on Keating himself, especially after his elevation to the prime ministership at the end of 1991. Keating's arrogant dismissal of popular unease, and his barely concealed message of "Trust me, I know what's good for you," earned him widespread antagonism from those on the margins of the globalised society. Paul's legacy was Pauline.

In transforming itself from a party of social democracy into a party of neo-liberalism, Labor had to reconcile itself with its historical ally, the trade union movement. Unlike in Britain, where the unions were attacked by the Iron Lady and then, severely weakened, outmanoeuvred by Tony Blair, the reconfiguration was achieved in Australia by way of the industrial Accords, negotiated under the prime ministership of Bob Hawke, former president of the Australian Council of Trade Unions. Aimed at moderating inflation and increasing employment, the Accords were a compact between the Labor government and the union movement in which the latter agreed to deliver industrial peace and moderate wage demands in exchange for political influence and, in later versions, tax cuts and improvements in the "social wage".

The Accords were negotiated in the midst of a long period of decline for trade unionism, a more or less continuous fall in membership from a high point of around 55 per cent of employees in the mid-'70s to less than 23 per cent now. It is a collapse attributable to structural change in the economy, the rise in part-time work and a perception among workers that unions are no longer relevant, especially with the replacement of awards with enterprise bargaining. Increasing affluence left many workers wondering about the value of union membership and the relevance of their "workerist" culture.

The decline in numbers has been matched by a decline in militancy. The effect of the Accords was to depoliticise the trade union movement. To be sure, it tied wage rises closely to a process of negotiation with the Labor government, but it also institutionalised the activities of the movement in a way hitherto unknown. The effects became apparent soon after the fall of Labor in 1996: having tied its future to a social compact with a sympathetic government, the union movement was left stranded, with a membership that had lost touch with its traditions of grass-roots radicalism.

This was a momentous shift. Twentieth-century Australia is sometimes said to have been built on the foundations of the "Australian Settlement", the trifecta of tariff protection, White Australia and arbitration. The interests of trade unions were at the centre of each of these elements. Perhaps a fourth element could be added: the social democratic idea that governments should commit to full employment that emerged after the Second World War. With cross-party consent, White Australia was abandoned in the 1960s, and the dismantling of tariff protection was begun by the Whitlam government and largely completed by governments of left and right over the next two decades. The commitment to full employment was in effect repudiated after the economic shocks of the early 1970s.

This left the entrenched social compact of post-Federation Australia teetering on one leg, that of arbitration. The Accords kicked it away. They marked the decisive shift in the enduring relationship between the trade unions and the social democratic party, a shift that culminated symbolically in the fiasco of the 2004 federal election campaign in which one powerful segment of the nation's most militant union, the CFMEU, vigorously backed the conservative government against Labor. Three days out from the election, the lead political story around the nation was the meeting of John Howard with Tasmanian timber workers. Promising to protect jobs that Labor would sacrifice to urban environmental sentiment, the Liberal Prime Minister was greeted with tumult and handshakes. If the fate of social democracy was sealed in 1983, perhaps this was the day on which it was finally interred.

A THIRD WAY?

Elsewhere in the world, the undermining of the foundations of social democracy played out in other ways. In June 1999 Tony Blair and German Chancellor Gerhard Schroeder together presented a famous paper entitled "Europe – The third way/Die neue Mitte". By laying claim to "the New Centre", it aimed to reinvigorate progressive politics in the aftermath of Thatcher and the New Right.

The Blair–Schroeder paper was a way of throwing down the gauntlet to so-called "traditionalists" in their own parties. In one fundamental respect the paper was right: the world had changed and social democratic parties had no choice but to reinvent themselves. But the question many traditionalists now asked themselves was this: could they stomach being reinvented as agents and facilitators of the free market, identical in many respects to their conservative opponents?

To the right of the new centre was the First Way, in which the principal objective of government was to reform the economy to maximise opportunities for private firms to create wealth and to promote personal choice. To the left was … what? As the Berlin Wall had crumbled a decade earlier, it was not clear what the Second Way could be except social democracy itself.

The Third Way is no longer the subject of polite conversation, but its fleeting prominence in the late 1990s is worth reflecting on for what it reveals about the larger question of social democracy. After all, for a couple of years it was a banner under which Blair, Schroeder, the Dutch prime minister, Wim Kok, and even Bill Clinton met in the hope of rescuing progressive politics from being swallowed whole by neo-liberalism.

As this alliance might suggest, the central ideas of the Third Way remained slippery. Some attempted to define it as a philosophy with three cornerstones:

the idea that government should promote equal opportunity for all while granting special privilege to none; an ethic of mutual responsibility that equally rejects the politics of entitlement and the politics of social abandonment; and, a new approach to governing that empowers citizens to act for themselves.

While this trio of aspirations corresponded with the pronouncements of Britain's Labour government and Germany's Social Democrat government, it was also entirely consistent with the emerging views of modern conservative parties. Although presented as the "renewal of social democracy", the Third Way accepted that the best way to achieve this objective was through the free operation of private markets. Anthony Giddens, the foremost academic advocate of the Third Way, conceded that in some situations constraints must be placed on markets, but this in no sense implied criticism of the free market as such. It is not inconsistent to accept the prevailing system and at the same time put forward policies to ameliorate some of its negative social and environmental effects, as long as one believes that the undesirable effects are not caused by anything fundamental to the system.

Unlike social democracy, and even more unlike democratic socialism, the philosophy of the Third Way was not based on any critical analysis of modern capitalism, or any alternative vision of society. In fact, it appeared to be defined by this absence, and a corresponding emphasis on managerialism. In contrast to traditional social democratic and socialist programs, one searches in vain the writings of Third Way luminaries for any mention of classes, exploitation, the influence of the profit motive, the power of transnational corporations, the division of labour, the dangerous side-effects of free markets, the alienation of consumer society, or even the root causes of unsustainable development.

The aversion to such criticism meant that advocates of the Third Way shied away from discussion of the motive force of political and social change – that is, the sources, forms and distribution of power.

Traditionally, socialists understood power to derive from ownership of capital, and oppression, injustice and inequality to arise from the struggle between capital and labour. Although most would now agree that this is a simplification that conceals as much as it reveals, it nevertheless focused on something fundamental in the structure of society. But in the Third Way no fundamentals were challenged; the world of the Third Way was characterised by complexity rather than conflict, and it is difficult to avoid the conclusion that talking about complexity served as a means of avoiding discussion of conflict.

Political ideologies – whether social democratic, conservative or liberal – provide a set of overarching political principles and a vision of society. Political parties find in them a template and a rationale for their decision- and policy-making. Yet the advocates of the Third Way argued that the pursuit of an ideology is old-fashioned, that society today is not marked by class division but by a "messy plurality", and that politics is no longer the art of struggles for class dominance and social transformation. Instead the politics of struggle has been superseded by the politics of lifestyle and the real concerns of "life politics" involve questions of equality of opportunity and the right to self-expression. As I will discuss later, there is some truth in this perception of modern attitudes and politics, but the problem was the uncritical acceptance of "life politics" by advocates of the Third Way. There was no analysis of *why* questions of lifestyle now dominate, and no discussion of whether the messy plurality is a surface manifestation of deeper, systemic social changes. The Third Way seemed to be saying that if people want lifestyle that is what we must give them, without asking what forces lie behind the pursuit of identity and self-worth through lifestyle choices and brand association, or critiquing how these perceptions are created and manipulated in a consumer society.

The triumph of neo-liberalism and the New Right in the 1980s coincided with the observation by social commentators that the people had lost interest in politics and that this apathy posed a threat to democracy. Hoping that the Third Way would rouse the public from its lethargy,

Giddens wrote: "Political ideas today seem to have lost their capacity to inspire and political leaders their ability to lead."

Yet the loss of political idealism bemoaned by Giddens was itself the product of the convergence of social democratic and conservative politics. The "life politics" of the Third Way was precisely the politics that best suited the consumer society. When questions of systemic injustice or entrenched conflict arose, the Third Way had nothing to say, and in this sense it was at one with the managers and the marketers, the corporations and their publicists, in its avoidance of the true business of politics – at least politics as conceived by the social democrats of days past. Nowhere in the writings on the Third Way can one find analysis of the larger social structures that shape the society in which people live; nor of the possibility of transforming these structures, or the obstacles to doing so. The political superficiality of the Third Way was the ideal counterpart to the emptiness of modern consumer capitalism. And, it must be said, the implicit social analysis of the Third Way still underlies Labor politics today.

Having accepted the fundamentals of the First Way, the Third Way was very soon characterised as little more than "Thatcherism with a human face". Many social democrats felt they could do little more than fight a rearguard action as, one after another, the pillars of the post-war social democratic consensus were knocked down. As socialism and state ownership became indefensible anachronisms, no coherent left alternative emerged. By contrast, the neo-liberal policy establishment, the network of think-tanks, business advisory bodies and educational organisations, grew ever stronger. Instead of searching for a creative response to the new dispensation, many of the most influential social democrats simply surrendered and embraced neo-liberalism – an assessment confirmed in 2002 by Peter Mandelson, often seen as Tony Blair's svengali, when he declared, "We are all Thatcherites now."

As opposition to privatisation, free trade, competition policy and deregulation of the financial sector fell away, the conservative and social democratic parties were more and more distinguished by means of prod-uct differentiation rather than ideology. Product differentiation and brand loyalty being marketing concepts, political parties began to hire market-ing specialists to help them sell their messages. And in the same way that clever marketing is required to persuade sceptical consumers that one brand of margarine is radically different from other, essentially identical, brands, ingenious methods were required to persuade sceptical voters that a political party was radically different from its opponents.

Increasingly, modern social democracy became the politics of politi-cians who are not sure what they stand for but who employ advertising agencies to convince the public that they stand for something. Today both conservative and social democratic parties complain that their opponents have stolen their policies. And they are right: so little that is fundamental separates the major parties that almost any policy can be found in the platform of their rival. The adoption of a particular policy is determined not by its consistency with ideology but by whoever thought of it first.

Thus the new leader of the British Conservative Party, David Cameron, has decided that if the Tories cannot outflank Tony Blair from the right, they will do so from the left. He has begun a policy review designed to soften his party's stance on immigration, appeal to Green voters (includ-ing promotion of organic farming) and win over female constituents by condemning the fact that women still do not receive equal pay. With the help of the rebellious knight Sir Bob Geldof, he has set out to prove that Tories can be more compassionate when it comes to global poverty than Tony Blair's Labour. The new strategy follows the failure of the old – the right-wing populism urged on the Conservative Party by the former cam-paign adviser of the Australian Liberal Party, Lynton Crosby.

In Australia, as in Britain, politics has made the transition from ideas to personalities. The spin doctor has replaced the policy analyst; the party platform can be found buried beneath the media strategy; image manage-ment has been substituted for bold reform; and choosing words has become more important than choosing actions. The fading of a substantive difference between the conservative and social democratic parties means that both are more likely to attract careerists and opportunists. We now see rising to prominence younger politicians who in their twenties were courted by both sides. They could comfortably have jumped either way, and have made their choice on the basis of which party would better facilitate personal advancement. Brendan Nelson is a case in point. As a former Labor supporter, his political pliability was apparent early and so it came as no surprise when he discarded his liberal social outlook along with his earring in order to join John Howard's cabinet. Now that he is mentioned as a potential prime minister one day, Nelson's decision to side with the conservatives appears a judicious one, although one sometimes suspects that his angry public defensiveness reflects an inner sense of self-betrayal.

Curiously, Nelson's successor as president of the Australian Medical Association, Kerryn Phelps, seems to fall into the same category. On her retirement, when asked if she planned to go into politics, Phelps said that she was considering it. Asked which party she would join, she said she had not yet decided. No journalist noted the irony. If she was not predisposed, by political principle or instinct, toward one or other party, but could comfortably fit into either, on what basis would she make a choice other than personal advancement?

The absence of any challenge to consumer capitalism meant that much of the Third Way's political agenda of the late 1990s was adopted quite comfortably by conservative parties, parties that, in some European countries at least, moved back from a hard-line position as the damage inflicted by the decade of neo-liberal policies became an electoral liability. The absence of any distinctive rationale for Third Way governments led Anthony Giddens himself to make the astonishing admission that they were making practical policy decisions unguided by any political principles:

> In the UK, as in many countries at the moment, theory lags behind
> practice ... governments claiming to represent the left are creating
> policy on the hoof. Theoretical flesh needs to be put on the skeleton
> of their policy-making ...

Usually, the skeleton that holds up the body would correspond to the theory and the policy detail would flesh it out, but the meaning is clear: we know what we want to do, but we lack a justification for doing it. Although Giddens was writing in the late 1990s, no progress has yet been made towards putting theoretical flesh on the policy bones and the attempt to "renew" social democracy has been abandoned, leaving daylight visible on the other side of the skeleton.

The Third Way came from nowhere, sparkled briefly in the political firmament and then winked out. Its function is now clear. It provided an ideological vehicle – a cover story – for former social democrats who had decided to abandon the ideas of the past but did not want to be seen to have cast their lot with the conservatives. The agents and advocates of the Third Way remained outwardly faithful to social democratic principles, but free of any obligation to past practice. Then, when it proved impossible to find a rationale for the new politics, the idea of doing so was quietly dropped. The debate had been won and there was no more need of cover.

From its origins, the Australian Labor Party saw its task as pursuing in the political domain what the unions sought to achieve in the industrial domain: it would constrain the power of capital and advance the interests of the working class. Social democracy was constructed on a class view of the world, one that, as long as it was not interpreted rigidly, remained germane throughout much of the twentieth century. The working class was defined, roughly but effectively, as composed of those who worked for wages (or piece rates in some industries). The bosses, their managers and the professional classes were more or less distinct. The politics of class reflected economic interests.

But in the 1970s and 1980s this well-defined worldview was shaken as the economy was transformed from one built on manufacturing, farming and mining to one dominated by service industries. The number of manufacturing jobs declined sharply, from 26 per cent of the labour force in 1966 to 14 per cent in 1995. The disappearance of the traditional base of the unions and working-class politics was matched by the rise of white-collar professionals. At the same time, the new social movements were creating a different way for individuals to look at the world. In the words of the German sociologist Ulrich Beck:

> Industrial society, understood as a model of the lifeworld in which gender roles, nuclear families and classes are interlocked, is disappearing ...

Today, while four out of five participants in the labour force remain wage and salary earners, class as a political category has virtually disappeared. This has eroded the rationale of social democracy as a political ideology. The idea of the working class, while formally defined in terms of its relationship to the means of production, was always inseparable from material deprivation and exploitation in the workplace. It was through the experience of deprivation that class consciousness had political potency. It is now clear that being allocated to the working class on the basis of one's relationship to the means of production is meaningless in the presence of affluence. But the argument goes further. Not only are those remaining in poverty, or significant material hardship, a small minority of the population, it is also no longer tenable to argue that their deprivation is an inherent part of the economic system. In his book *Beyond Left and Right*, David McKnight reminds us that poverty is generated at the level of the family and is associated with family breakdown, substance abuse, mental illness and poor education. While these misfortunes do tend to be concentrated in some groups, it makes no sense to attribute them to class divisions.

This is not to say that inequality in the distribution of income, opportunity and power has disappeared; far from it. But the concerns that motivated social democracy — poverty, inequality and exploitation — are, as a result of affluence, now confined to a small proportion of the population, no more than 20 per cent. While the moral imperative to improve the circumstances of this group remains — indeed, in the face of widespread affluence, it has even greater force — the circumstances of 20 per cent of the population cannot provide the basis for a politics of social transformation in the twenty-first century.

When I addressed the ALP Left conference in 2002, I was accused of ignoring and abandoning the poor. The claim that less than a fifth of the population of a country like Australia is prone to material deprivation therefore needs to be backed up, not least because many social democrats continue to work from a base assumption of widespread material deprivation. It is this worldview that I had to confront with the facts in 2002, and which leads some now to accuse me of being blind to the "real world" of ordinary Australians. In 2004–05 the typical, or median, level of disposable income for all families with children in Australia was $50,500. The average disposable income is higher than the median. But before saying more about the extent of true hardship in Australia, it is vital to distinguish between real and imagined deprivation.

The perception of widespread deprivation is real enough, but the actuality does not match the belief. In fact, a large proportion of Australians who by any historical or international standard are wealthy believe themselves to be doing it tough. This is largely due to the fact that although real incomes have been rising rapidly, aspirations have been rising faster still. More so than in previous eras, we have become accustomed to judging our living standards with reference to the lifestyles of those around us, and, increasingly, those presented to us by advertisers and television producers. Yet when people reach the financial goals they have set for themselves, they feel no happier. Instead of wondering whether the yearning for more money is the problem, they raise the amount of money they believe they need to satisfy their desires. This is a vicious circle. In part it continues because it is not the absolute level of income which affects our wellbeing but the relative amount: it's no fun being twice as rich if everyone else is twice as rich too. In fact, studies have shown that most people would prefer an income of $50,000 where the average is $40,000, to an income of $70,000 where the average is $100,000; that is, most people would rather be poorer, provided others are poorer still.

The persistence of imagined deprivation was illustrated by a Newspoll survey commissioned by the Australia Institute in 2002. When asked, 62 per cent of those polled said that they could not afford to buy everything they really needed. When we consider that Australia is one of the world's richest countries and that Australians today have real incomes three times higher than in 1950, it is remarkable that so many people believe their incomes to be inadequate. It is even more remarkable that when the results were broken down by income group, almost half of the richest 20 per cent of households in Australia – the richest people in one of the world's richest countries – said that they could not afford to buy everything they really needed.

Another study, using data from the Household, Income and Labour Dynamics in Australia (HILDA) survey, found that only 5 per cent of millionaires in Australia regard themselves as prosperous, while more than half say their financial situation is only "reasonably comfortable". Even among the very wealthy — those with household net worth in excess of $3 million — only one in five regard themselves as prosperous, while 7 per cent say they are "poor" or "just getting along".

Much the same pattern emerges when income (as opposed to net worth) is the criterion. Only 5 per cent of those living in households with incomes above $100,000 describe themselves as prosperous. At the other end of the spectrum, only 9 per cent of those in the lowest income group (less than $25,000) say they are "totally satisfied" when asked about their financial situation. But exactly the same proportion of those in the highest income group (over $100,000) say they are totally satisfied.

As this suggests, it is vitally important to distinguish between imaginary hardship (which is widespread) and real hardship (which is not). Recent studies help us understand the extent of real hardship. A nationwide survey by the Australian Bureau of Statistics asked the following question:

> Over the past year have any of the following happened to your household because of a shortage of money?

The results — reported in Table 1 — found that on average 16 per cent of households could not pay their gas, electricity or telephone bills on time. This included 5 per cent of the households with the highest incomes. Although wealthy households can experience cash-flow problems that make them late in paying their bills, it is fair to assume that the stress caused by the inability to pay bills on time is much greater among the poorest households. On the other hand, any household forced to pawn something, to go without meals or home heating, or to seek assistance from a welfare organisation, is experiencing genuine hardship. It is noteworthy, though, that even in the very lowest income group only about 10 per cent of households are so affected, and across the whole population perhaps only 3 or 4 per cent fall into this category. There could be other markers of genuine hardship that the Bureau's questions did not pick up, but even so it appears that a substantial majority of households in the

Table 1. Items that households went without, by quintile (%)

	Total	Household income quintile (equivalised)				
		Q1(low)	Q2	Q3	Q4	Q5(high)
Could not pay gas/electricity/ telephone on time	16.1	23.4	22.5	17.6	11.7	5.2
Could not pay car registration/ insurance on time	6.5	8.8	7.9	8.0	5.6	2.3
Pawned or sold something	4.2	7.9	6.4	3.6	2.5	0.8
Went without meals	2.7	6.5	3.7	1.7	1.3	0.3
Unable to heat home	2.2	5.1	3.6	1.4	0.8	0.3
Sought assistance from welfare/ community orgs	3.5	7.5	5.7	2.6	1.2	0.3
Sought financial help from friends/family	9.9	14.6	13.3	9.6	8.5	3.6

Table 2. Items that households cannot afford, by quintile (%)

	Total	Household income quintile (equivalised)				
Cannot afford:		Q1(low)	Q2	Q3	Q4	Q5(high)
Week's holiday away from home each year	27.3	44.0	38.0	29.6	17.7	7.3
Night out once a fortnight	19.4	31.2	28.9	21.7	11.3	3.9
Friends/family over for a meal once a month	5.3	11.1	9.5	3.5	1.9	0.4
Special meal once a week	11.6	22.6	17.2	10.8	6.0	1.6
Brand new clothes (usually buy second-hand)	11.8	23.4	19.7	9.6	4.6	1.4
Leisure/hobby activities	9.1	18.1	14.0	7.9	4.4	1.1

Source: Rob Bray, *Hardship in Australia: an analysis of financial stress indicators in the 1998–99 Australian Bureau of Statistics Household Expenditure Survey*, Occasional Paper No. 4, Department of Family and Community Services, Canberra, 2002, Table 1. Household income quintiles have been "equivalised", in other words, adjusted to account for the number of adults and children in each household. If the first adult counts as 1, the second counts as 0.5 and each child counts as 0.3.

lowest income group does not report hardship of this kind. As the analyst, Rob Bray notes, "while lower-income households have, on average, higher levels of [financial] stress, many of these households experience no financial stress at all."

As one would expect, in the highest income group the incidence of genuine hardship is virtually zero. Yet nearly half of this group say they cannot afford to buy everything they really need. It is fair to conclude that, using any reasonable definition of "needs" and "basic necessities of life", a substantial majority of Australians who experience no real hardship believe they are "doing it tough". We might be tempted to dismiss this as merely an unfortunate delusion on the part of the people concerned. However, the notion that large swathes of the population are suffering some form of deprivation is one of the underlying suppositions of political debate and policy formulation in Australia. Among other things, it provides the basis for the political appeal of middle-class welfare and tax-cutting auctions at every federal election. The imagined hardship of today is a parody of the class consciousness of workers that drove the development of social democracy in this country.

A second study, also based on ABS data, focused on access to "extras" rather than basic necessities. The survey asked respondents whether they could afford to spend money on items such as annual holidays, a night out and hobbies. By looking at specific behaviours rather than general attitudes to financial circumstances, the survey elicited information about whether households actually go without certain items. Table 2 shows the proportion of households in different income quintiles that say they cannot afford certain things. With the exception of new clothes, the items in question – holidays away, eating out, having friends for a meal, and hobbies – cannot be considered physical necessities, although most would be regarded as essential to a reasonable standard of living in Australia today. Social inclusion, being able to participate in society, is important to well-being as any child whose parents cannot afford to send them on a school excursion well knows.

In the case of items such as a week's holiday away (which 27 per cent say they cannot afford), a night out once a fortnight (20 per cent) and having friends around for a meal (5 per cent), the proportion of households saying they cannot afford these activities is relatively low compared with the general belief of 62 per cent of households that they cannot afford to buy everything they really need. Even so, these claims have to be taken with a grain of salt: almost one in five households in the second-highest income group claims that they cannot afford a week's holiday each year, although 56 per cent of the poorest households say they can. Even among low-income households, only about 20 per cent say they have to do without special meals, new clothes and leisure activities, which means that around 80 per cent of these households can afford these items.

These studies help to put the extent of poverty in Australia into proper perspective. Australia's foremost poverty researcher, Peter Saunders of the Social Policy Research Centre, has recently summarised the state of play. His best estimate is that around 12 per cent of Australians can be said to be living in poverty. This, however, represents the numbers living in poverty at any one time. The numbers of those living in entrenched poverty from one year to the next are substantially lower, perhaps half that number, with the rest accounted for by those whose income falls below the poverty line for a limited time. Some are university students who will become affluent.

Although there may be no agreement on whether 5 per cent or 15 per cent of Australians live in poverty, it is untenable to maintain that the principal social problem confronting modern Australia is widespread material deprivation. Yet it is difficult for many people to admit that their lifestyle would have been viewed as luxurious by their parents or grandparents. This reluctance can in part be explained by a dual discourse that dominates the public domain. On the one hand, advertisers appeal to consumers' desire for luxury ("Go on, pamper yourself, you deserve it"); on the other, politicians and the media keep alive and cultivate the myth of the Aussie battler.

In an earlier era Australia *was* a nation of battlers, of working people who were hardened by the rigours of economic depression and war, and, if not proud of their penury, certainly not ashamed of it. The Aussie battler became the central icon of Australian political folklore, and the image persists into the present even though, as a result of sustained economic growth in the past five decades, the number of people who truly struggle has shrunk to a small proportion of the population. For every genuine battler there are three or four who imagine they fit the description. That is why our political leaders keep alive and exploit the myth of the Aussie battler.

Hansard, the verbatim record of the Federal Parliament, shows that in the 18 months from January 2003 to August 2004 politicians referred to "battlers" 237 times, "struggling families" 54 times and Australians "doing it tough" 65 times. This could simply reflect politicians' propensity to speak in clichés, but even so the choice of clichés is revealing. One senior minister even referred to battlers who earn more than $60,000 a year. Another referred to the tax cuts of the 2003 Budget – which went overwhelmingly to high-income earners – as rewarding the battlers.

The place of the Aussie battler in the national psyche is reinforced by the media. A Commonwealth Bank survey of savings behaviour in 2002 concluded that 60 per cent of Australians were finding it hard to cover their living expenses, a big increase on the previous year's 48 per cent. The bank described these people as "struggling". Media reports interpreted the survey results as confirmation that the bulk of the population is finding it difficult to make ends meet. In Canberra, one of the wealthiest areas of Australia (and the world), the local newspaper led with, "Almost half of all Canberra households are struggling to cover their living expenses, let alone save for a rainy day, new research has shown." The article went on to discuss the position of the lowest income groups who depend on charity, as if the circumstances of people living in poverty are equivalent to those of middle-class mortgagees: "The figures have alarmed local welfare and charity groups, who believe the trends could push more residents into financial crisis."

A similar message was delivered by a series of prominent stories in a Sydney newspaper. Under the headline "Families sucked into mortgage nightmare", the paper reported on a "crisis in housing affordability", with one in five households in "mortgage stress". The tenor of the articles was that large numbers of Sydney residents found themselves under financial pressure because of the size of their mortgage repayments as compared with their incomes. Expressions such as "people with mortgages are hurting", "crisis looms", "problems have undoubtedly become more severe" and "real hardship areas" serve to reinforce the popular impression that most Australians are doing it tough and are trapped in a difficult situation that is not of their making.

Yet the "mortgage stress" that generated the headlines is not the unexpected result of rising interest rates or falling incomes: it is the result of luxury fever, which has driven many thousands of individuals to borrow more money than they can comfortably repay in order to satisfy their escalating acquisitiveness. In other words, many people have set their sights on levels of comfort and luxury they cannot afford and have taken on too much debt in order to get there. The newspaper reports fail to distinguish between, on one hand, poor households in genuine difficulty because they cannot afford rising rents even in poorer suburbs and, on the other, wealthy households in mortgage stress as a result of $600,000 mortgages on large houses in wealthy suburbs.

Previously, when wealthy people made the decision to live beyond their means, their financial difficulties attracted little public sympathy. If they complained, it might be suggested that they consider living a little less grandly. Today, newspapers, commentators and political leaders depict the imagined financial difficulties of the wealthy as the result of hard times rather than inflated expectations. The problem thus becomes a matter of public concern. The real concerns of yesterday's poor have become the imagined concerns of today's rich.

Some will react to these observations by claiming that, in arguing that its incidence is not as extensive as is widely believed, I am trivialising the problem of poverty. In fact my intention is to counter the opposite tendency, that of talking up the extent of poverty in order to emphasise its moral and social urgency as a problem to be addressed. Too many social democrats adopt this tactic in the mistaken belief that inflating the problem will stimulate greater public sympathy and more government action. But it has quite the opposite effect: if everyone is struggling, there is nothing unique about the poor. And a middle class convinced that it is living in straitened times is more likely to vote for middle-class welfare, such as family payments and private health insurance rebates, than for poverty alleviation. Exaggerating the extent of deprivation also locks social democrats into an anachronistic understanding of the world, one whose foundations have been destroyed by decades of sustained economic growth, and this in turn prevents them from developing a progressive political vision that resonates with the times.

As affluence increases, class ceases to be a useful category: its explanatory power diminishes, and fewer people find it a meaningful category in their own lives. The political implications of this have been far-reaching. Most obvious has been the extent to which the Labor Party's grip on the votes of the traditional working class has been released, as reflected in the emergence of the class of voters known as "Howard's battlers". The Liberal treasurer, Peter Costello, can get away with claiming that we are now all working class only because the concept has been deprived of its meaning.

In traditional social democratic politics, a well-defined working class saw the ALP as the party that could advance its economic interests in the political domain through institutions that would protect working conditions and fair wage levels. It would also provide public services such as schools and good health-care that would improve opportunities for working people. The Labor Party is still more likely to protect the interests of low-income people by measures such as these. The Coalition government's changes to industrial relations laws, greater financial support for private schools, rising fees for university education and massive subsidies for private health insurance all penalise low-income families in one way or another. But it is also true that the majority of employees will be little affected by the changes to the industrial laws, large numbers of workers have private health insurance, and half send their children to private high schools or aspire to do so. The constituency for whom social democratic policies were traditionally designed has shrunk dramatically.

In 2004 a woman rang a Perth talk-back program to insist that her family would be worse off under federal Labor's tax policies. She was soon outed for failing to declare that she was a paid-up member of the Liberal Party and had served on the party's state executive. She later said that, having declared on radio that her household's income was only $32,000 a year, she was embarrassed when her friends in the Liberal Party found out that her family lived "close to the edge". It does not seem remarkable today that a suburban housewife from a low-income family should join the Liberal rather than the Labor party. (In fact the woman, who glories in the name Mrs Poor, later capitalised on her talkback notoriety by obtaining Liberal Party preselection for a state seat.)

The radical changes that undid the social democratic contract in industrial relations, private school funding and so on were implemented by the Hawke-Keating Labor governments of 1983–96. Today the ALP is promising merely to stop the conservatives from finishing the job it began. Telstra was the only major public utility under Commonwealth control that the Hawke-Keating governments did not sell off, and not for want of trying. Enterprise bargaining and the erosion of the award system was a Labor initiative. Labor vastly increased public support for private schools and introduced HECS (although the latter measure had good equity arguments in its favour). While Labor vehemently opposed the Coalition's introduction of the GST in 2001, a decade before Keating had failed in his push to introduce the same tax.

No wonder the electorate is confused. Now, when Labor attempts to differentiate itself by a return to traditional principles of social justice (as occurred with the proposal at the last federal election to shift some funding from elite private schools to poorer ones), it finds that most workers no longer identify with these sorts of issues because they have risen above the lowest levels of pay and aspire to much more. We have not yet reached the situation of the United States where, as someone said, "there are no people living in poverty in the USA, only millionaires temporarily down on their luck," but that is where we are heading.

Nor should the willingness of the conservatives to adapt their policies be underestimated. Last year, an analysis by the National Centre for Social and Economic Modelling showed that contrary to the widely held belief that the poor are getting poorer and that the Howard government has abandoned them to their fate, the average real income of the bottom 20 per cent of families with children increased by the same proportion (18 per cent) as did that of the average family over the seven years to 2004–05. The figures are accurate; they reflect the system of targeted family payments refined by the Coalition. We now have the bizarre spectacle of the Labor Party attacking the Coalition for being the highest-taxing government in Australian history, and then promising to reduce taxes by more than the conservatives. This has gone so far that senior Labor figures, including union leader Bill Shorten (spoken of as a future Labor Party leader), have called for a reduction of the top marginal tax rate to 30 per cent, into which bracket the incomes of his members apparently fall. Voters are perfectly right to ask: "What does Labor stand for?"

For most thinkers of the Left, lack of justice, however it is conceived, remains the defining characteristic of modern capitalist society, and the primary focus of those who aim to create a better society is to overcome injustice. For some social democrats, the foundations of injustice lie in the nature of capitalism: economic pressures to inequality must be countered by political activism designed to bring greater fairness to the system. For others, injustice is located in the domain of culture: it will be defeated through social change as well as political activism. Whether inequality is conceived in terms of distribution of resources or treatment of individuals and groups, it is the struggle against injustice that defines and gives enduring relevance to social democracy.

Against this, I maintain that the defining problem of modern industrial society is not injustice but alienation, and that the central task of progressive politics today is to achieve not equality, but liberation. Social democracy as we understand it cannot deliver this goal and a new politics is required.

There is no question that before the Second World War, and indeed into the 1950s and 1960s, industrial capitalist societies were characterised by extensive and severe injustices. A large percentage of the population experienced material deprivation, especially during economic downturns, and protecting and advancing the material interests of wage earners was the paramount consideration. Moreover, all aspects of public life – economic, social, political and cultural – were dominated by a structure of distribution and recognition that was designed to give a privileged place to white men.

Political theorists of the Left made a persuasive case that both of these forms of injustice were inherent to the structure of capitalism. Thus, put crudely, subjugation of working people was essential to sustaining profits and investment; unpaid women's work was the unseen foundation on which the market economy was built and keeping women in the kitchen was necessary to sustain that economy; and suppression of racial minorities was necessary in order to provide a continuing supply of low-wage workers for the most menial jobs.

Yet this attribution of economic injustice and minority oppression to the structure of capitalism proved to be wrong. While the battles have been fierce and problems remain, this way of characterising capitalism in rich countries like Australia is no longer defensible. If this is true, the principal problem of capitalism is no longer injustice.

In recent decades, in the rich countries of the world, the forces that held in check the material aspirations of working people have for the most part fallen away. In the post-war decades, not only did incomes treble but mass education saw class barriers crumble. And the liberation movements of the 1960s and 1970s tore down the oppressive structures that constrained the lives of women and minorities. The sexual revolution freed us from our Victorian inhibitions; the women's movement freed women from role stereotyping; gay liberation allowed free expression of sexual preference; and the civil rights movement eliminated institutionalised racism.

I am not arguing that all problems have been solved and injustice no longer exists. That is patently not true. Three manifestations of injustice continue to blight our society.

First, poverty remains present in Australia, with around 10 to 15 per cent of the population at any one time suffering significant material deprivation. This is manifestly unacceptable and is all the more unconscionable because it persists in a land of affluence.

Secondly, the circumstances of many indigenous Australians are a matter of national shame. Indigenous people no longer experience institutionalised discrimination, land rights have been granted and extensive attempts have been made by governments to provide social services and income support. Yet it must be said that the remedies prescribed by social democracy appear to have had little impact on the parlous state of many indigenous communities.

Thirdly, the members of one minority group, those people with physical disabilities, despite important forms of progress, continue to suffer neglect. In a country like Australia, people with disabilities are perhaps the last minority genuinely feared by the majority.

So yes, injustice and discrimination continue to exist. But – and this is my fundamental point – they cannot be understood as structural characteristics of modern capitalism. It is perfectly feasible to imagine a social and economic structure in all essentials the same, but in which poverty is much diminished, the circumstances and opportunities for indigenous Australians are vastly improved, and people with disabilities are respected and cared for.

The fact is that neo-liberalism has fulfilled its promise of prosperity, delivering large increases in income across the board. It is simply untrue that the rich inevitably get richer and the poor get poorer. Over the last thirty years there have been periods when income inequality has declined, and there have been periods when it has increased. The difference is in part due to the activity of governments, with periods of falling inequality usually, but not always, coinciding with the tenure of social democratic governments. This is a continuing struggle and there is little doubt that the Howard government's changes to industrial relations laws will see wages at the bottom falling, thereby worsening income inequality, unless there are increases in welfare provision or tax credits are introduced to compensate, neither of which measure is out of the question.

In addition, the liberation movements have long since won the culture war. If we imagine ourselves back in 1965, listing all of the demands of these movements, which were then in their infancy or still to emerge, I think we would have to admit that 80 per cent of what was envisaged then has since been achieved. Consider the case of women's equality. Almost all of the institutional barriers to equality have been dismantled, and discrimination on the basis of sex is now outlawed. While the process is not complete, women have made enormous strides, with perhaps the most striking statistic being that female students now outnumber males at universities, and do so across most disciplines. The most prestigious professions, medicine and the law, are now being feminised. To be sure, work remains to be done. Inequality in wages remains in some areas, in part due to the residual legacy of discriminatory attitudes. But even here evidence suggests that lower pay for the same work is in part due to the preference of female employees to bargain for better conditions instead of higher pay, whereas their male counterparts are fixated on pay scales.

It is often observed that the division of domestic labour is still a problem, with men refusing to do their fair share of housework so that working women are compelled to do a double shift. Undoubtedly the cultural shift required of men by feminism has been slow in coming, but at the same time there has been a backlash against the intense social pressure on women to emulate the traditional male model of career and full-time paid work throughout a working life. While men do not do their fair share of housework, many women have come to the view that it is a mistake to believe that in every type of household a fair share means an equal share. Compared with the gender divides that marked, say, the 1950s, women are now in a vastly superior position to negotiate with their male partners a fairer distribution of paid and unpaid work in the interest of the household, taking into account the preferences and predilections of both parties. The labour market now offers a plethora of opportunities for women and it tells us a great deal about their inclinations that the enormous influx of women into the labour market has been dominated by one fact: the preference of half of them to work part-time.

Thus, for the most part, the great social movements of the 1960s and 1970s have transformed the life circumstances of women, gay men and lesbians and people of minority ethnic origin, permitting them the opportunity to be recognised for who they are. But alongside this something profound and barely noticed has occurred. After the institutionalised forms of discrimination were swept away, a deeper, more insidious crisis of identity has become apparent. The problem of identity is no longer centred on the recognition of minorities, it is a majority concern, and the threat to authentic selfhood is not the oppressive attitudes and actions of a dominant group. The threat to identity today derives from a different, more diffuse and far more insidious source – the market itself.

What is the nature of alienation, which I argue is the defining problem of modern consumer society? For all of the promises of the liberation movements, it cannot be maintained that the mass of people today have been freed to realise their full potential and achieve fulfilled and meaningful lives. The subjugation of the human spirit in consumer culture manifests itself, to an ever-increasing degree, in restless dissatisfaction, chronic stress and private despair, feelings that give rise to a rash of psychological disorders – anxiety, depression, substance abuse. We engage in a range of behaviours aimed at compensating for or covering up these feelings.

It was not meant to be like this. When the new social movements rejected traditional standards, expectations and stereotypes, it was a manifestation of the deeper human longing for self-determination. The democratic impulse – which until the 1970s took the form of collective struggles to be free of political and social oppression – had metamorphosed into something else, a search for authentic identity, for true individuality. At last, here was the opportunity for the mass of ordinary people to aspire to something beyond material security and freedom from political oppression. Before we had an opportunity to reflect on our new-found freedom, however, and to answer the question "How should I live?", the marketers arrived with their own answer to the quest for true identity.

Over the last two or three decades, the agents of the marketing society have seized on the primal desire for authentic identity in order to sell more gym shoes, cars, mobile phones and home furnishings. And what has happened at the level of the individual is echoed in society's preoccupation with economic growth, an autistic behavioural pattern reinforced daily by the platitudes of the commentators and the politicians.

Today, most people in rich countries seek proxy identities by means of commodity consumption. The hope for a meaningful life has been diverted into the aspiration for higher incomes and increased consumption. Why do we succumb? We continue to pursue greater wealth and consume at ever-increasing levels because we are afraid of the alternative. The yearning that we feel for an authentic sense of self is pursued by way of substitute gratifications, external rewards and, especially, money and material consumption.

Advertising long ago discarded the practice of selling a product on the merits of its useful features. Modern marketing builds symbolic associations between the product and the psychological states of potential consumers, sometimes targeting known feelings of inadequacy, aspiration or expectation, and sometimes setting out to create a sense of inadequacy in order to remedy it with the product. When consumers are at the point of making a purchase, they are subliminally asking themselves two questions: Who am I? Who do I want to be? These questions of meaning and identity are the most profound questions humans can pose, yet today they are expressed in the lines of a car and shape of a soft-drink bottle. The advertising industry demands such creativity of its employees because the creeping sense of failure associated with consumption requires continual invention of new ways of appealing to the need for personal identity.

The task of the advertising industry is to uncover the complex set of feelings associated with particular products and to design marketing campaigns to appeal to those feelings. This is a challenge: consumers, for the most part, do not consciously understand what they want or why they want it. Prodigious intellectual and creative effort is poured into marketing, driven by the imperative of consumer capitalism. All aspects of human psychology — our fears, our sources of shame, our sexuality, our spiritual yearnings — are a treasure-house to be plundered in the search for a commercial edge. Thousands of the most creative individuals in societies such as ours devote their lives to helping corporations manipulate people into buying more of their brand of margarine or running shoes at the expense of another corporation selling a virtually identical product.

The beauty of this approach is that consumers can never get what they want. Products and brands can never give real meaning to human lives, so consumers lapse instead into a permanent state of unfulfilled desire. This, of course, is the essential state of the consumer in modern capitalism. Thus shopping has become the dominant response to the meaninglessness of modern life. Consumption is no longer an act by which we satisfy our needs but a means to acquiring a "lifestyle" that conforms with the type of person we want to be. Consumer spending has changed from an activity aimed at acquiring status through displays of wealth to one of creating the self through association with certain products and brands. We no longer want to keep up with the Joneses; we want to trump the Joneses by differentiating ourselves from them. It is virtually impossible today to buy any product that is not invested with certain symbols of identity acquired by the buyer knowingly or otherwise.

The process is an insidious one. When buying a Toyota Camry some years ago, I was conscious of my desire not to be sucked in by advertising images and associations and wanted a vehicle that said as little as possible about myself. Then last year I heard an advertising executive say on radio that the Toyota Camry is designed to be purchased by people who want to communicate to the world that they are an "understated type of person". One cannot win.

The demands of the baby boomers for freedom in private life, for freedom from the fetters of convention and for freedom of sexual expression were noble in themselves, but it is now evident that demolition of the old social customs and moral rules did not produce a society of free individuals. Instead, it created an opportunity for the marketers to substitute material consumption and manufactured lifestyles for the ties of social tradition. In the face of revolutionary changes in social attitudes in the West, consumer capitalism has remained unruffled. Indeed, each new social revolution has provided an opportunity for it to rejuvenate itself.

This development has been most apparent in the women's movement. The opportunity provided by gender equality for women to find their real selves has been co-opted by the market. Incipient recognition of this fact has led to a questioning of the feminist project. In her 1999 book *The Whole Woman*, Germaine Greer expressed her dismay at where feminism had ended up. For all the advances in education and employment, and for all the dramatic alteration in attitudes, women have now become paid-up members of the market system. They have achieved equality so that they can feel alienated and exploited in the way men do. They sought liberation but settled for equality. Greer might have gone further and said that women wanted liberation but were bought off with equality. Women can never be liberated until men are too, and neither can be free while they are active and willing participants in consumer culture. In the 1950s, middle-class respectability may have been oppressive but it carried with it a certain deference. Women are the subject of far more sexual objectification now than they were in the 1950s, first with "girl power" and now with "raunch culture" and the pornographication of everyday life.

Feminism has been co-opted. "Women's liberation did not see the female's potential in terms of the male's actual," wrote Greer. "[T]he visionary feminists of the late sixties and early seventies knew that women could never find freedom by agreeing to live the lives of unfree men." In fact, women's liberation turned out to be a superb marketing opportunity. Here was a huge new demographic that wanted something different — commodities that would express how the new woman felt about herself.

Gender equality has meant unfettered opportunity for women to create themselves in the images invented for them by the marketers. Whether a woman is a dutiful housewife or a kick-arse careerist is a matter of indifference to the marketers, so long as she continues to spend. There is no difference between an advertising campaign that appeals to the image of the nurturing, caring mother and one that targets the power-dressed professional; indeed, the cleverer campaigns manage to combine both. Each identity is merely a demographic; the only difference is that the independent professional believes she is more in control of her life when she is deciding what to buy.

*

The shift in the 1960s from a politics of inequality to a politics of identity involved a new focus on the cultural and social domain, rather than on underlying economic forces. In an unexpected way, however, the position I am advancing, which stresses the central place of identity and alienation in modern consumer capitalism, returns to an economic explanation. In the process, what we understand by the "economic" has changed. Social democracy and socialism emphasised the relationship of individuals to the means of production. Today it is not production but consumption that is the key, in particular the relationships of individuals to the goods they buy and the influence of marketing in the formation of those relationships. Problems arise from the penetration of the economic into the social and cultural domain. By this I mean both the spread of private firms into new areas – childcare, welfare provision, public services – and the spread of the values of market – commodification, individualism and competition – into areas of social and cultural life from which they were previously excluded, such as education, the arts, sports, charitable activities and domestic work.

Although the ideal of justice is losing its political force, this does not mean that power, exploitation and alienation have disappeared; rather they have re-emerged in a new guise. Previously, a concern for justice gave rise to demands for greater equality (fairer distribution of income and wealth, or equal treatment of excluded groups); today, tackling the new forms of exploitation and denial of identity involves controlling, regulating or eliminating the power of the market. The answer is no longer equality; it is liberation.

There is still progress to be made in the social democratic project – retaining workplace protections, fine-tuning the welfare state, protecting civil liberties, and sustaining the fight against racist and homophobic attitudes. These tasks are not trivial, but it is a characteristic of political struggles that the benefits of the changes demanded are exaggerated and golden futures are promised. Exaggeration is an irresistible rhetorical device, but the danger is that the protagonists come to believe their own rhetoric. We readily recognise this among those committed to causes that we do not share, especially causes that most see as trifling or wacky. Those who campaign vehemently against fluoridation of water come to mind, yet for these activists fluoridation is not just a grave threat to public health but a profound attack on civil liberties.

Social democrats preoccupied with the residual problems of welfare capitalism and with the battle against the erosion of past gains must answer this question: If all of their demands were granted tomorrow, would we have a society with which we could be satisfied? If we protected workplace conditions, fixed the welfare state and did all we could to promote reconciliation, would that be enough? Is the prevailing system with a few of the rough edges knocked off all we can hope for?

For me it's not enough. I don't believe such a society could provide the conditions for citizens to lead contented and fulfilling lives. In other words, the successes of social democracy do not mean that suffering has been abolished; indeed, I suggest, the clearing away of the constraints of poverty and discrimination have only permitted the deeper sources of discontent under consumer capitalism to make themselves felt.

Not long ago, while walking through Sydney's CBD at lunchtime, I over-heard a snippet of conversation between two young women sitting in the sun. "I'm not sure what to do with my life," said one. It struck me as a very modern statement, implying that the young woman had in front of her myriad possibilities and that the responsibility for deciding which path to take was entirely her own. In the 1950s, by contrast, few young men and women would have asked themselves "What will I do with my life?" Then, the options facing most appeared limited. For a young work-ing-class man the question was likely to be, "Which trade would I do best at?" Middle-class men had greater room to move, although the option of choosing a trade rather than a white-collar occupation was proscribed by social expectations. For young women the choices were even more restricted. For most the future was largely mapped out. The idea that the world was at their feet and they were free to choose to do whatever they liked would have seemed entirely alien. There was a word for people who thought like that – "irresponsible" – and if such people insisted on defy-ing all expectations and conventions, they would in all likelihood end up outside normal society, becoming bohemians or something even less acceptable. In other words, social expectations and constraints relieved individuals of much of the personal responsibility for determining their own life-course that weighed down upon the young woman basking in the sun that day.

The young woman used the term "my life" as if it were a discrete entity that belonged to her alone, which starts and ends and in between follows a course that is determined largely by herself. That idea of "my life" to which we are now so strongly attached is the quintessential product of the liberation movements of the 1960s and 1970s, whose aim was above all to destroy those social expectations, norms and constraints that prevented individuals from making their own lives. The women's, sexual liberation and civil rights movements were demands for self-determination built on the belief that everyone, and especially those oppressed due to their gender, race or sexual orientation, should no longer have their life choices constrained by social taboos, discriminatory beliefs or their class background. The arguments that raged through those years were about "rights", and above all the right of individuals to make their own life choices unhampered by convention, tradition or prejudice. The social movements gave everyone the opportunity to ask: "What will I do with my life?"

Ulrich Beck has argued that, in place of societies in which people form their sense of self by unconsciously absorbing the cultural norms and behaviours of those around them, living in largely homogeneous neighbourhoods and communities, we live in an era of "individualisation". The term refers to the requirement to create one's own self, to "write one's own biography" instead of having it more or less drafted by the circumstances of one's birth. The new imperative arises in a society saturated by the outpourings of the mass media, in which the symbols of achievement and the characters worthy of emulation appear on the screen and the magazine pages rather than in the local community or in handed-down stories of the saintly and heroic. Whether individualisation is a blessing or a curse — whether it means the final step to personal freedom or being set adrift from all that is solid — is not the point; the point is that fixity can no longer be assumed, that personal relationships and connections to social groups are always contingent, that individuals must now scan the world to decide with whom or what they wish to identify. The process of individualisation creates the social conditions for the flourishing of modern consumerism by providing the opportunity for the marketers of goods to step in and capture the yearning to find and express a self. Increasingly, it is to the market, to the brands and the lifestyles attached to them, that people turn in order to create themselves — not to their communities, clubs or unions. And, as I have described, in this world it is consumption, as typified in shopping, that becomes the characteristic act. This has had two profound effects on how people think about themselves, each with far-reaching consequences for modern politics.

The first is that instead of being products of our life circumstances, individualisation has meant that we have come to accept that we are each of us responsible for our own life. Those who succeed in socially sanctioned ways feel justified in their efforts and duly rewarded for their dedication, determination and superior character. Their success absolves them of the need to feel compassion for those who have failed, for failure can only reflect poor choices or a lack of character. Those who do not succeed must internalise their disappointment rather than blame the bosses, the schools, the government, exploitation or "the class system". In this world, social problems become individual failures; there are no more dysfunctional societies, only individual "losers", a process that has a deeply conservative political effect.

It is worth noting that a society of this kind does not necessarily prescribe dog-eat-dog individualism for all of its members. The opportunity to chart one's own life-course does not mean that we must inevitably choose to be self-focused. Indeed, any new progressive politics must navigate this gap; it must be a politics that persuades citizens in an individualised society to consider others before oneself, and to do so in the face of the overwhelming injunction of consumer culture and the market to do the opposite. On the other hand, because we live in an "individualised" society, not simply a society of rampant and selfish individuals, any "communitarianism", preaching a return to social homogeneity, is inescapably utopian; it cannot work.

The second effect of individualisation is that the replacement of class-based stratification by a collection of individual life stories has, paradoxically, a homogenising effect. The identities that can be forged out of the products provided by the market are not to any great degree the creations of those who adopt them, but are rather manufactured by "popular culture" and thus controlled and co-opted by marketing. Thus the individuality of the marketing society is a pseudo-individuality, as if there were an invisible hand guiding the pen that each of us takes up to write our biography.

The nature of the individual has also been transformed. Social democracy saw the individual as a member of a class engaged primarily in an economic struggle, from which was derived an identity and a place in the social order. Today's individual is free-floating; no longer subject to material privation, his or her choices are vastly expanded, at least in principle. Many people could choose to step off the materialist treadmill and distance themselves from the influence of the market. This is why the phenomenon of downshifting — representing that fifth or so of Australians who have voluntarily decided to reduce their income to pursue life goals other than material accumulation — is so momentous.

It is the argument of this essay that the compulsion to participate in the consumer society is no longer driven by material need or by political coercion, but by the belief of the great mass of people that to find happiness they must be richer, irrespective of how wealthy they already are. If ordinary people today are exploited, then it is by common consent. They choose the gilded cage and would prefer not to be told that the door is open. Thus, in rich countries today the power of the market is primarily an ideological rather than an economic one.

As a consequence, the old idea of solidarity, the emotion that powered social democracy, has little meaning. People are no longer drawn together by their oppression, united against a common enemy, or bound by a shared cultural history. In place of solidarity, they aspire to occupy a position superior to that of their peers, or at least to differentiate themselves from them, so as to assert their unique individuality. Because consumer capitalism and neo-liberal ideology have succeeded so spectacularly in creating the impression that each of us is a self-made individual, the widespread acceptance of social justice has evaporated. Australians are far less likely now than three decades ago to have sympathy for the poor, and much more likely to attribute their disadvantage to the personal inadequacies of those so blighted.

Can Labor reinvent itself as a social democratic party, or as a party with a progressive political stance that distinguishes it in a substantive way from the conservatives? Its recent history provides a few signs that it may be able to do so. Among the thinkers in the party there is an incipient recognition that the old model can no longer serve the interests of the party or the nation. Soon after he was elected leader in February 2004, Mark Latham gave a speech at the National Press Club. The media reported him as calling for more male mentoring, but this was only mentioned in passing in the speech. A bigger theme, which was almost completely ignored, was Latham's acknowledgment that giving priority to the economy will not necessarily make Australians any happier. Declaring that there is more to life than money, he emphasised the importance of strong relationships to our wellbeing and acknowledged the desire of most Australians for something more meaningful than a pay rise and a bigger house.

> As we become more prosperous as a nation, people are demanding that our prosperity has a purpose beyond the accumulation of more possessions. Increased wealth in a society does not necessarily make us happier.

The speech signalled his growing doubts, yet he soon returned to his themes of aspirational politics and the ladder of opportunity which dominated the election campaign in October 2004. But by the time he wrote his *Diaries* – which for their searing insights will in my view become one of the most important documents of modern Australian politics – his view of Australian society appeared to have shifted to one very close to the one I articulated to the conference of the ALP/Union Left.

> Traditionally [he wrote], Left-of-Centre parties have tried to achieve their goals for social justice by tackling various forms of economic disadvantage. Today, however, the biggest problems in society ...

tend to be relationship-based — social issues, not economic ones. The paradox is stunning: we live in a nation with record levels of financial growth and prosperity, yet also with record levels of discontent and public angst.

He went on to mention some of the evidence for this and returned throughout the book to the themes of self-centred materialism and the "gulag of consumerism".

> All the messages in our public culture push people towards materialism: commercial advertising, the glorification of wealth, keeping up with the Joneses. The middle-class response to an unhappy life is further consumption, the temporary escapism of material goods.

In his Introduction to the *Diaries*, Latham made the striking admission that his stress on aspirational politics had been a mistake. He had since come to understand that aspirational voters turn into selfish mortgagees preoccupied with their own financial circumstances and with little concern for their communities.

> People live in highly geared McMansions, on $60–$70 000, couple of kids at a non-government school, and they say to the politicians, "I'm the real battler, help me ..."

Similar views have been expressed in recent years by a number of other senior Labor figures. In his 2002 *Quarterly Essay, Beyond Belief*, former Hawke-Keating minister John Button restated the traditional deprivation model of social democracy but also expressed doubts about the "aspirational voter". He wrote that these are people who are desperate to get ahead, with big mortgages, kids at private schools and four-wheel drives, all paid for by two parents working excessive hours. "There is little point accumulating more and more wealth and enjoying it less," he opined. Yet his discussion of signposts to the future carried little conviction that the Labor Party could renew itself.

In his 2003 book *Crowded Lives*, Lindsay Tanner, the current shadow minister for finance, took up the same theme of "affluence fatigue".

> We're on a treadmill that's imperceptibly gaining speed. To buy all these things that save time we have to work more. We've created a vicious circle of time consumption, where the cost is borne by our relationships.

Carmen Lawrence, a former president of the ALP, has made similar arguments and, more recently, leadership contender Julia Gillard has spoken of the "ailments of affluence", suggesting that there exists a yearning for social solidarity.

> When there is a quiet but emerging debate about the limits of commodity fetishism as a source for happiness, something's going on. When there is a small but clear movement of people to "downshifting", something's going on. When evangelical churches that provide a whole of lifestyle engagement with others are growing rapidly, something's going on ... This yearning for connection should not be underestimated as a powerful political force for change.

These are tentative steps towards a new political debate, taken by thinkers from both the Left and the Right of the Labor Party. Tempting though it is, however, it would be a mistake to read too much into them. None of these Labor thinkers has nailed their colours to the mast, advanced an alternative vision and forced the party to engage in a new debate.

It may be that the Labor Party is now structurally incapable of accommodating a wide-ranging and radical debate. The new theme, beginning to be developed by the Labor figures I have mentioned, has not even drawn criticism; it has simply been ignored as irrelevant to real politics. This dismissiveness can in part be attributed to the anti-intellectualism of the Australian press, and especially the parliamentary press gallery, the herd mentality of which makes fools of otherwise intelligent people.

Labor Party factions once served as a means of organising to promote ideas that were held passionately by their members. As Mark Latham describes to devastating effect in his diaries, these factions now divide only notionally along ideological lines. They have become vehicles for ambition and mutual support. If a contest of ideas cannot be carried out through the factions, where in the party can it occur? Perhaps the federal parliamentary caucus should be reorganised to create an Ideas faction which could then engage in a war for the party's soul with the Opportunist, Careerist and Deadwood factions, conservatives one and all, who would resist change to the last. Another entrenched "faction" which would need to be defeated is that of the party machine itself, which has in recent years been the object of severe criticism from senior party members, including Barry Jones, John Faulkner, John Button and Carmen Lawrence.

I had a taste of its disdain for ideas when I received an invitation to speak at an "ideas forum" at the 2004 ALP National Conference, held at Darling Harbour in Sydney. Although sceptical, I took the invitation as a sign that the Labor Party, or at least some in its organisation, believed that it needed new ideas and policy debate. Like the other speakers on the panel – Barbara Pocock of the University of Adelaide, a specialist in work and family policy, and Evan Thornley, the internet entrepreneur who has decided to devote his time and fortune to reviving social democracy in the Labor Party – I had put considerable effort into thinking about what I could most usefully say in the twenty minutes allocated to me.

Arriving on the day it was difficult to find our session on the conference program, and my doubts about the seriousness with which it was to be taken were heightened by the allotted venue – a vast but otherwise empty convention hall, with a few dozen chairs arranged in a corner. Perhaps forty or fifty people turned up. As we were about to be called to the stage, an ALP functionary approached to inform us that things had changed and we had now no more than five minutes each, "preferably less". My fellow panellists had also prepared a twenty-minute talk and travelled interstate at their own expense. The message was clear: the Labor Party had no real interest in engaging with ideas but wanted to create the appearance of being open to fresh thinking. This conclusion was symbolically reinforced when I took the podium. The preceding event had been a presentation to teenagers by Labor luminaries, which had now turned into a photo-op three metres from the stage. My truncated talk was drowned out in the hubbub, and the audience could not help but watch the smiles and flashing cameras. The chair of the session, Wayne Swan, sat stonyfaced and unconcerned, seemingly interested only in getting the whole event over and done with as quickly as possible.

In a way this small incident reveals the true state of modern Labor. In a party divided into hardened factions and sub-factions whose principal purpose is to promote the ambitions of their members, leadership contenders are required to feign an interest in policy ideas and social change, sometimes by writing a book to demonstrate their credentials. Of course, the capacity to put ideas into the public realm is severely constrained because every MP has been drilled on the damage that any perception of "disunity" can do. Having an idea that can be construed by the media as being contrary to party policy is a dangerous thing in the modern Labor Party. The press gallery is in some measure to blame for this, for it long ago decided that no idea should be treated on its merits, but rather considered solely for its possible political impact. Yet if disunity is death, it is nothing compared to the *rigor mortis* of dull conformity.

In his *Diaries*, Latham describes the suffocating impact of the factional system. What he writes has been confirmed by many others with detailed knowledge of how the party operates. There is one glaring anomaly in the overall argument of Latham's book, however, and it demands an explanation. The party that he so sharply condemns is the same one that elected him as leader. It is possible that Latham stood out as a potential leader because of the flatness of the surrounding countryside; yet everyone knew that he was a high-risk choice. His election revealed a hidden aspect of the Labor Party that has received little attention.

Despite the oppressiveness of the factional system, it seems there are enough members of the Parliamentary Party willing to buck the factional bosses if the circumstances are right. The attraction of Latham, sufficient to persuade a majority of caucus members to overcome their fears, was that he presented as a man of bold ideas. Support for the specific ideas Latham had articulated throughout his parliamentary career was limited; much of his Third Way analysis was unpersuasive and some of the policy ideas garnered little support. But he was the man with ideas. Politics is about seizing the initiative, and it is through ideas that this can be achieved. The Latham election indicated that there is a subterranean recognition, even within the Parliamentary Labor Party, that the old social democratic model is no longer tenable, and yet neither is the strategy of emulating the Liberal Party. The willingness of Labor's caucus to elect Mark Latham as party leader was perhaps the only sign of hope for the future of the ALP as a party of social reform. His demise, due at least in part to the conservatism and control of the factional bosses, has meant a retreat to the reactionary politics embodied in the figure of Kim Beazley.

Yet there is an air of unreality about the debate over factionalism. The problem is characterised as a purely institutional one. The debate is wholly inward-looking, as if the problem lies solely with a handful of power-hungry factional bosses who, through organisational cunning, have managed to capture the party. The structural problems of the party are rarely debated in historical terms, so no one asks what has been happening in Australian society that has allowed the ALP to be transformed from a party built around a powerful set of values and social goals into one dominated by personal fiefdoms. Thus the "radical solutions" for reform include reducing union representation at national conferences and banning parliamentary staffers from seeking preselection until they have had "real jobs" for at least two years.

The problems of the party structure are manifestations of a wider malaise — ideological convergence, individualisation in society, the withdrawal from politics and the withering away of solidarity. The party that evolved to represent the interests of trade unionists and their families cannot survive in a world where union membership has shrunk to less than a quarter of the workforce and where those who remain have been depoliticised. As David McKnight has argued, unionism is now but one of several broad social movements, and just as a political party built on environmentalism or feminism could not provide an alternative vision and organisation to challenge the conservative party for government, nor can one with its roots in unionism and which is controlled by union bosses. Internal party reform would be meaningless without a wholesale re-invention of the party's social base, philosophical rationale and platform. It is pointless debating organisational reform without first debating philosophical renewal.

The Australian Labor Party has served its historical purpose and will wither and die as the progressive force of Australian politics. There is no better sign of this than the mostly vacuous series of papers analysing Labor's 2004 election defeat published by the worthy but anachronistic Fabian Society. None of the contributors, with the exception of Guy Rundle, had anything sharp or new to say. Evan Thornley wrote about "our people" not trusting us, as if there were a mass of people out there yearning for the Labor Party of old, yet called for a new "brand" for the party. Bill Shorten, the union leader with politics somewhere to the right of Chopper Read, argued that Labor must now move to the centre! That would be a move to the left. He roundly rejected any severing of the connection between the ALP and the unions, and called for tax cuts for high-income earners and businesses. Judith Brett bemoaned the inward focus of ALP luminaries, then concluded that the way forward is to change the rules for preselecting candidates. John Button, the elder statesman, at least spared the reader nostalgic references to that greatest of Labor clichés, the light on the hill. The lack of direction in the essays, or any clear-headed analysis of what the problem is or where Labor might go, was dispiriting to say the least.

Although his diagnosis of the problem is very acute, the answer to

Labor's malaise is not that given by Mark Latham in a lecture to Melbourne University students in September last year. "The system is fundamentally sick and broken," he said, "and there are other more productive and satisfying ways in which you can contribute to society." A withdrawal from organised politics altogether can only leave the main stage to the conservatives. For one such as Latham, schooled in Labor politics from his teenage years, a retreat from the Labor Party means a retreat from politics. Others see the need to build a progressive alternative to the Labor Party. Still others have joined the Greens; yet as a third force aspiring to become the second force of Australian politics, the Greens are hamstrung by three facts.

First, the party's origins in environmentalism, and continuing emphasis on environmental issues, limit its ability to appeal to a wider audience, despite extensive attempts to broaden its platform. Its name doesn't help. The Greens, however, have become a powerful force in local government, the natural home for a party of its orientation and structure.

Secondly, the charisma and moral authority of Bob Brown is perhaps the greatest asset and the greatest weakness of the Greens, and his departure will severely test the enduring appeal of the party.

Thirdly, the party has some serious organisational and cultural handicaps, including a large number of activists who are emotionally and ideologically wedded to fringe politics and who work against the broadening of the Greens' appeal. This is especially true in New South Wales, where the party is controlled largely by a clique whose methods are reminiscent of Trotskyists.

Yet as the last decade of conservative rule has reminded us so painfully, an effective, electable progressive political party is vital to the promotion of social progress and the protection of Australian democracy. All of this points inescapably to the need for a new political party founded on a philosophy and an organisation that reflect the contemporary world.

From the late 1990s a growing body of evidence has challenged the foundational assumption of modern politics, that more economic growth is the key to continuing social progress. This body of evidence is now so robust that it has undermined the rationale of the whole neo-liberal project; at the same time, it has challenged the assumptions on which social democracy was constructed. A number of psychologists, and a few economists, have for several years been surveying citizens of rich countries asking them how they feel about life. It has became clear that they are not happy in themselves. An analysis of the condition of US society in a major report commissioned by the Merck Family Fund in 1995 is particularly striking. Titled *Yearning for Balance*, it reached four important conclusions.

First, Americans believe that the value system that dominates their society is wrong, that "materialism, greed, and selfishness increasingly dominate American life, crowding out a more meaningful set of values centred on family, responsibility, and community". The vast majority want their lives to be based on values of family closeness, friendship, and individual and social responsibility, yet they believe their society fails to promote these values.

Secondly, Americans believe that materialism has overtaken society, with dire consequences; that "lust" for material things lies at the root of crime, family breakdown and drug addiction. Four-fifths believe they consume far more than they need to and are concerned about the inability of people today to save for the things they want. Children are considered to be especially possessed by a corrupting materialism.

Thirdly, Americans are ambivalent about the contradiction they face. They can see that materialism is corroding society and themselves, but wedded to "financial security" they are too fearful to change their behaviour in any significant way. They therefore avoid too close an examination of their own behaviour, yet the contradiction gives rise to a deep conflict of conscience.

Finally, Americans understand, albeit somewhat vaguely, that rampant consumerism is destroying the natural environment. There is an overwhelming concern that the world left for their children will be less safe and less secure and will have the wrong value system.

It took a while for me to grasp the political implications of both this research and the swathe of papers produced by psychologists pointing out that more materialistic people are less happy. Then it struck me: the neoliberal revolution had always been justified on the grounds that the freeing of markets would be good for the economy, and that getting the economy to grow as quickly as possible is the best way to increase social wellbeing. Yet there was a gaping hole in the argument: freeing markets may get the economy growing faster, but that will not necessarily make people any happier.

Yearning for Balance demonstrated that in the United States, the nation that epitomises growth fetishism, the growth project has for the most part failed to improve people's lives. It is not simply that other trends in society, occurring in parallel with rising incomes, have offset the benefits of wealth: the process of promoting economic growth itself has produced a seriously sick society. The richest people in the world are saying they are miserable, that it's not worth it and, most disturbingly of all, that it is the process of getting rich that causes the problems. Continued pursuit of material acquisition gives rise to inner conflicts that become manifest in society in various ways, and this helps to explain some of the major social problems that cause so much community concern.

The *Yearning for Balance* report found, in stark contrast with the optimism of the post-war boom, a pervasive sense that things could only get worse, that the future was bleak. I decided to test whether this was also true in Australia and commissioned Richard Eckersley to prepare a report on *Quality of Life in Australia: An analysis of public perceptions*, which was published in September 1999. In addition to reviewing a range of evidence, the paper reported the results of a new survey commissioned from Newspoll. At a time of high income growth, low unemployment, low interest rates and general economic stability, it found that only 24 per cent of Australians believed that the quality of life in Australia is getting better (and of those, 18 per cent said only a "little better"). Over a third (36 per cent) said life is getting worse, while slightly more (38 per cent) said that it was staying about the same. Eckersley also asked respondents in which decade they thought quality of life in Australia was highest. Only a quarter nominated the 1990s. Eckersley concluded:

> Australians are looking for a different national and social vision ...
> What polls are measuring, and qualitative surveys are explaining,
> is a growing tension between values and lifestyle, a tension being
> heightened by the promotion of a fast-paced, high-pressure, hyper-
> consumer lifestyle on which current economic performance
> depends.

This new understanding of the postmodern world was also implicit in the Genuine Progress Indicator (GPI). First published in the US and applied here by the Australia Institute, the GPI is an alternative to Gross Domestic Product as a measure of national progress. It incorporates more than twenty aspects of economic welfare excluded or wrongly measured in GDP, including the value of household work, the costs of crime and traffic congestion, and various measures of environmental decline. Initially calculated for the period 1950–97, and updated in 2000, the GPI told a story about post-war progress radically different from the one suggested by GDP growth. While tracking GDP quite closely through the 1950s and 1960s, in the 1970s the GPI began to slow and then fall, even as GDP per person continued its inexorable rise, interrupted only by periodic recessions. The conclusion was plain: the costs of growth had begun to outweigh the benefits.

These facts, and the story they tell about life in modern consumer capitalism, present a devastating challenge to neo-liberalism – one that neo-liberals still have not worked out how to respond to. At the same time, they undermine the deprivation model which is the basis of social democratic politics. After all, both neo-liberalism and social democracy assume that the health of the economy is the foundation of social progress.

The last three decades have witnessed a dramatic change in the forces that govern society. In the case of capital, modern firms are driven less by competition through cost-cutting and more by product differentiation and marketing. The spread of affluence and the transition to consumer capitalism have meant that identity now has less to do with one's work — where one is placed in the production process — and more to do with one's consumption choices, including consumption of cultural products.

This view of the world can be represented in the following ten propositions. They apply only to affluent countries, although the consumption behaviour of rich consumers in poor countries has some of the same characteristics.

Ten theses on consumption

1. In rich countries, the principal purpose of consumption spending is no longer to satisfy needs but to find and express a personal identity.

2. For a large proportion of consumption behaviour, the act of buying and the act of consuming have become distinct and need to be understood separately.

3. Marketing, including advertising, is designed to get us to buy, not to consume, and where possible prefers us not to consume but to discard.

4. There is an inexorable process of converting wants into "needs" and this results in and reflects a ratcheting up of expected standards of living, one in which expectations always stay in advance of incomes.

5. Because of the limits to consumption capacity, this ratcheting-up process inevitably results in more waste.

6. The rise in expectations or aspirations puts pressure on people to work longer and harder and this comes at the cost of their personal relationships.

7. Whereas growth in consumption was once necessary to improving wellbeing, in rich countries increased consumption is now associated with declining wellbeing.

8. Improving wellbeing today requires a partial withdrawal from the market and a distancing from its influence, including an active resistance to the market values of materialism, competition at the expense of co-operation, individualism and the money-metric.

9. The trend towards voluntary reduction of incomes and consumption, known as downshifting, is a reaction against the pressures of consumerism.

10. A shift to a society based on a downshifting ethic and the associated rejection of consumption as the basis of lifestyle and self-definition is the only way to gain an authentic identity and, incidentally, protect ourselves from severe environmental decline.

It is my contention that these ideas provide the basis for an alternative progressive politics, one which resonates with the life circumstances of citizens of affluent countries by building on an understanding of how consumer capitalism has transformed the world and how it has influenced the way we think about ourselves and our lives.

Such a progressive politics would speak to the underlying concerns and longings of Australians across all parts of the community. Public awareness of the cost of consumer lifestyles has given rise to an inner conflict between what we do daily and what we believe is right for us and our society. A large majority of Australians believe that escalating materialism has harmful effects. According to a survey taken in December 2004, 80 per cent agree with the proposition, "Most Australians buy and consume far more than they need: it's wasteful." This view is strongly held across all income and age groups. And there is widespread concern about the effects of overwork on the quality of family life, with 75 per cent of Australians agreeing with the proposition "Too many Australians are focused on working and making money and not enough on family and community" (a concern treated with disdain by the new industrial relations legislation pushed through by the Howard government). Once again, with the partial exception of respondents aged over seventy, this view is held strongly across all income and age groups, and especially strongly by women.

Australians seem particularly troubled about the corrupting effect of materialism on children. Four in five believe strongly that Australia's materialistic society makes it harder to instil positive values in children. This explains why 86 per cent believe greater limits should be placed on advertising to children, including 47 per cent who strongly agree with this. The widespread desire to put barriers between advertisers and children undoubtedly reflects the enormously increased effort by advertisers to target children. Regardless of whether they are parents or not, Australians believe that materialism is harmful to children and that simple steps such as curbing advertising should be taken. Typically, the response of governments and the advertising industry is to suggest that parents take more individual responsibility for what their children are exposed to. But parents cannot opt out of society; they cannot control everything their children see and do; nor do they want to. Parents feel overwhelmed by the responsibilities governments impose on them and know that taking collective action to protect their children is the best way to make a difference. When governments refuse to accept responsibility for providing collective solutions, they ensure that the problem will persist.

Most Australians, including those caught up in consumerist lifestyles, feel the prevailing value system is warped. They believe Australia has become too selfish and superficial, that people have lost touch with the more desirable standards of personal behaviour such as self-restraint, mutual respect and generosity. Conservatives have been much more adept than progressives at tapping into these concerns, even though in the name of choice they promote the very market values and consumerist goals that corrode the values we seek.

The desire of most Australians for a society built on core human values has been twisted into support for a retrograde conservative morality including vilification of single mothers, hostility towards gay relationships and attempts to demonise the "undeserving" poor. The values of a decent society have been overlaid by outdated prejudices and positions based on particular religious convictions. And, responding to a pervasive sense of social disintegration, conservatives have made political gains by taking a disciplinarian stance on crime and drugs. The majority of Australians want to live in a society with greater moral certainty, stronger constraints on anti-social behaviour and clearer sexual standards; conservatives appear to offer solutions, even if those solutions are packaged up with other positions that many find uncomfortable.

Thinkers and leaders on the progressive side of politics have become wary of the new politics of morality, seeing it as the stalking horse of conservatives whose approach is often punitive, divisive and repressive. Schooled in the ethical universe of the 1960s and 1970s, when the assertion of minority rights saw the overthrow of oppressive rules, many progressives have failed to engage with the moral concerns of the citizenry and have abandoned to those on the political right the most fertile grounds for social change. Now that the laws and norms that imposed sexual repression, limited opportunities for women and sanctioned racism have been renounced, the Left has ended up standing for little more than the market economy with a bit of "social justice" thrown in. Defending minority rights is not a trivial task, but it should now be clear that it cannot form the basis of a progressive politics in the twenty-first century.

Nowhere are these contradictions more keenly fought out than in debates over the idea of the family. Promoting "the family" has become conservative territory, but it is time progressives muscled their way in with a new politics of relationships. Everyone wants a happy family life. Families are the source of most of the companionship, emotional support and love we experience throughout our lives; they are where we form our most enduring, caring and loyal relationships. Yet many progressive people, as if still crippled by the feminist and leftist critiques of the nuclear family, are afraid to defend the family; and, perversely, the more the moral conservatives have seized on the notion and moulded it into a romantic and reactionary caricature of the nuclear ideal of the 1950s, the more the progressives have vacated the field. This has been a political mistake.

The widespread unease with consumerism, even among the so-called aspirational classes, and the longing for a society with stronger values derives from something deeper than a perception of social decline. Like all humans, what modern Australians want above all is for their lives to have purpose. But finding meaning is not easy, especially when people are subjected to a barrage of commercial messages that promote superficiality, self-deception and instant gratification. Some are following a religious path, and join growing church communities where they can, for a time at least, immerse themselves in a social environment that is welcoming, caring, joyous and devoted to a higher purpose. This explains the proliferation of evangelical Christian churches, where the corrupting influences of consumer culture can be left at the door and people can participate unselfconsciously in a celebration of being together. They can find affirmation and value in being part of a community. This is a rare experience nowadays, but it fulfils an essential human need – one that television, shopping malls and political parties cannot meet.

Progressives feel uneasy about the importation of American evangelism, for good reason: these communities lend themselves to capture by conservatives who distort the participants' desire for a stronger moral order into an assault on outsiders who deviate from "the one true path". But, rather than deriding the "happy clappers" of the evangelical churches, we need to realise that it is only through understanding and accepting the urge to find something more satisfying than a consumer life that a "politics of meaning" can be built. Responding to most people's wish to live with purpose in an ethical society ought to be the natural territory of progressives, since the sentiments that underlie this yearning are consistent with the construction of a more just, sustainable and peaceful society.

The foregoing comments suggest a moral and philosophical basis for a new politics of wellbeing. A politics of wellbeing would give priority to fulfilling work and help citizens to reclaim their time. It would encourage vibrant, resilient, sustainable communities and help people develop the skills to build stronger family relationships. It would wind back the process of commercialising educational institutions and insist that schools and universities be devoted to improving the physical, emotional and moral health of young people, rather than certifying them for the workplace. It would not hesitate to counter the forces that spread growth fetishism, especially the barrage of deceptive marketing. It would recognise when the values of the market intrude into areas of life where they do not belong and − deaf to the self-interested cries for more "choice", "development" and "economic freedom" − take measures to exclude them. And the new politics would no longer be tempted to sacrifice the natural world to lift GDP by half a per cent.

These points in turn suggest a number of policies that could form the initial basis of a party platform:

- Provide fulfilling and flexible work through regulation of the labour market. Workplace flexibility, including quality part-time jobs, should operate in the interests of employees as well as employers.

- Acknowledge that work in the household is essential to the health and wellbeing of families and communities. Because it is outside the official economy, such work has, up till now, been ignored. Governments should value this work, and employers need to adapt to the realities of family life. Providing for generous maternity leave, paternity leave and carers' leave is essential.

- Transform educational systems so that they are dedicated to creating capable, confident, emotionally mature young people who are equipped to face life's vicissitudes. We should reverse the process of turning universities into businesses selling degrees and instead concentrate on making them places where students flourish as humans and academic staff feel free to question powerful institutions without fear of victimisation.

- Invest in early childhood. Shared parental leave should be extended to cover the first two years of a child's life.

- Promote responsible advertising. Advertisers prey especially on children because they know children lack the critical capacity to distinguish between facts and advertising fiction. As in Sweden, advertising to children aged less than twelve years should be banned, and advertising codes of conduct should be legislated so that irresponsible and deceptive marketing is outlawed.

- Protect the environment. We can do much more than we have done to date. We should move towards a system that increases taxes on damaging environmental activities such as burning fossil fuels and reduces taxes on socially beneficial activities such as providing fulfilling work. We should make the generation of waste very expensive and reward businesses and households that reduce their consumption and recycle materials.

- Measure what matters. We need a set of national wellbeing accounts so that we can monitor our progress. These accounts should report on the quality of work, the state of our communities, our health, the strength of our relationships, and the state of the environment. Governments should be judged by how much our wellbeing improves – not by how much the economy expands.

The new politics of wellbeing challenges the traditional parties equally because it says that, for all of the economic benefits of free markets, in the end we cannot find true happiness in a shopping centre. It sidesteps the traditional Left–Right debate over who can best manage the economy, and asserts that in rich countries the market has become the enemy rather than the friend of social progress.

The obstacles to the new politics should not be underestimated. Environmentalists have long recognised how difficult it is to persuade people to change entrenched consumption habits. Consumption behaviour and the sense of personal identity are so closely related that a challenge to someone's consumption behaviour is a challenge to their very sense of self. Green moralising and appeals to rational self-interest have taken us as far as they can. If it continues to rely on existing campaigning methods, environmentalism is doomed to fail for, in the absence of an appealing alternative, most people would sooner consume themselves to death than risk killing off the self they know.

It is not utopian to believe that citizens of the affluent West can be persuaded that there is a more authentic and fulfilling alternative to the consumer life. There are signs that, after decades of intensifying consumerism, many people are beginning to rebel. For example, when asked in a national survey whether, over the last ten years, they had voluntarily changed their lives in ways that meant they earned less money, 23 per cent of 30- to 59-year-olds said "yes". This figure, which excludes early retirees and new mothers, means that around one-fifth of the population has "downshifted" over the last decade; that is, they have voluntarily decided to reduce their incomes and consumption levels. Similar figures apply in Britain and the US and they have far-reaching political implications.

Although symbols of the reaction against intensified consumerism, down-shifters, and their cousins the "cultural creatives", are not for the most part motivated by philosophical concerns but simply want to get some balance back into their lives – to devote more time to their families, their health and their passions. They are choosing fulfilment over money or, as I said at the outset, rich lives instead of lives of riches.

A new progressive politics would build on the values and goals of this movement and set out to create social structures that support them – workplaces that provide fulfillment, communities that cultivate closer relationships, a culture that promotes true autonomy (the capacity to act according to internalised values and norms) in place of pseudo-individuality, education systems that produce self-aware and compassionate citizens rather than self-interested consumers, and public institutions that serve national wellbeing and democracy rather than imitate the culture of the market.

Not far beneath the surface most Australians have a gnawing doubt about the value of a money-driven life. In our national survey we found that, despite most respondents saying they can't afford to buy everything they need, more than four in five also believe that our society is "too materialistic, that there is too much emphasis on money and not enough on the things that really matter". They suspect that the money society is at the root of the decline in values – the disposable relationships, instant gratification, moral laxity, selfishness, corporate greed and the loss of civic culture.

It is in showing the link between the money society and the decline in values, and then painting a picture of a new society that is less selfish and materialistic and more devoted to the "things that really matter", that a new politics can be forged.

ACKNOWLEDGMENTS

I am greatly indebted to Robyn Eckersley, David McKnight and Frank Stilwell for reading a draft of this essay. While their comments have allowed me to improve it markedly, I have not been able to do full justice to their insights and they are not responsible for any views expressed here. I would also like to thank Chris Feik, the editor of *Quarterly Essay*, for excellent advice.

SOURCES

5   Labor's constitution: <http://www.alp.org.au/download/national_constitu
tion_2004.pdf>.

6   CSL sale analysis: C. Hamilton and J. Quiggin, *The Privatisation of CSL*, Discussion
Paper No. 4, The Australia Institute, Canberra, June 1995.

6   The term "animal spirits" was used by Keynes to describe the whimsical
nature of investor sentiment. Nowadays economists describe the phenomenon, in its manic phase, as "irrational exuberance".

14   "three cornerstones": this definition comes from the "New Democrats"
Progressive Policy Institute <www.ppionline.org>.

14   "constraints must be placed": Anthony Giddens, *The Third Way: the renewal of
social democracy*, Polity Press, Cambridge, UK, 1998.

15   "the real concerns of life politics": Giddens, *The Third Way*, p. 44.

16   "Political ideas today": Giddens, *The Third Way*, p. 2.

19   "theory lags behind practice": Giddens, *The Third Way*, p. 2.

20   Ulrich Beck, *Democracy Without Enemies*, Polity Press, Cambridge, UK, 1998,
p. 21.

21   David McKnight, *Beyond Left and Right*, Allen & Unwin, St Leonards, 2005,
p. 126.

21   "less than a fifth": in most of continental Europe and Japan the proportion
of the population prone to poverty and exploitation is less than that in
Australia, but in the US it is significantly higher.

21   "median of $50,500": Justine McNamara, Rachel Lloyd, Matthew Toohey
and Anne Harding, *Prosperity for All? How Low Income Families Have Fared in the Boom
Times*, National Centre for Social and Economic Modelling, University of
Canberra, 2004. The average disposable income of a family with two children in the bottom 20 per cent of the population was $28,800 a year. This
group is dominated by welfare recipients and includes a disproportionate
number of single parents.

22   "most people would rather be poorer": see, for example, Bruno Frey and
Alois Stutzer, *Happiness and Economics*, Princeton University Press, Princeton, NJ,
2002, p. 91.

22   Newspoll survey: Clive Hamilton, *Overconsumption in Australia: the rise of the middle-
class battler*, Discussion Paper No. 49, The Australia Institute, Canberra, 2002.

22   "three times higher": measured in 1990 constant dollars, GDP per person
was $9126 in 1950. By 2000, it was $26,755. Clive Hamilton and Richard
Denniss, *Tracking Wellbeing in Australia: The Genuine Progress Indicator 2000*, Discussion

Paper No. 35, The Australia Institute, Canberra, December 2000, Appendix Table 1.

22–23 Survey using HILDA data: Clive Hamilton and Claire Barbato, *Why Australians Will Never Be Prosperous*, Australia Institute Webpaper, July 2005.

23–25 ABS survey reported by Rob Bray, *Hardship in Australia: an analysis of financial stress indicators in the 1998–99 Australian Bureau of Statistics Household Expenditure Survey*, Occasional Paper No. 4, Department of Family and Community Services, Canberra, 2002.

26 Peter Saunders, *The Poverty Wars*, University of NSW Press, Sydney, 2005.

27 The six paragraphs commencing "In an earlier era ..." borrow from Hamilton and Denniss, *Affluenza*, Allen & Unwin, Sydney, 2005.

27 "Almost half of all Canberra households": *Canberra Times*, 6 August 2002.

28 "prominent stories in a Sydney newspaper": *Sydney Morning Herald*, 12 August 2002.

29 "we are now all working class": *Sydney Morning Herald*, 17 May 2005.

30 "She later said that": *Weekend Australian*, 5–6 February 2005.

31 real income increases: McNamara et al., p. 12 and Figure 11.

32 For debate about how to characterise injustice, see Nancy Fraser and Axel Honneth, *Redistribution or Recognition? A political-philosophical exchange*, Verso, London, 2003.

46 "Traditionally ...": Mark Latham, *The Latham Diaries*, Melbourne University Press, Melbourne, 2005, p. 12.

47 "All the messages": Latham, *The Latham Diaries*, p. 15.

47 "his stress on aspirational politics": Latham, *The Latham Diaries*, p. 16.

47 "People live ...": Latham, *The Latham Diaries*, p. 371.

47 John Button, *Beyond Belief: What Future for Labor?*, Quarterly Essay, Issue 6, Black Inc., Melbourne, 2002, p. 69.

48 Lindsay Tanner, *Crowded Lives*, Pluto Press, North Melbourne, 2003, p. 52.

48 Julia Gillard, "Of Lions, Tigers & Labor's Future", Speech at the launch of *Losing It* by Annabel Crabb, 28 September 2005, Parliament House, Canberra.

48 Public perceptions of *The Latham Diaries* were shaped largely by press gallery journalists, most of whom are represented in the book in an acutely unfavourable light. I now use the index in the *Diaries* as a quick guide to the press.

51 "radical solutions for reform": as suggested by reformers on *Background Briefing*, ABC Radio National, 5 February 2006.

52 *After the Deluge? Rebuilding Labor and a Progressive Movement*, Blue Book Special Issue, Australian Fabian Society Pamphlet No. 64.

53   Mark Latham, "Ten Reasons Why Young Idealistic People Should Forget About Organised Politics", Public Lecture by Mark Latham at the University of Melbourne, 27 September 2005.

54   The report may be found on the website of the New American Dream <http://www.newdream.org/yearning/yearn_full.html>. The study was based on a series of focus groups conducted across the US followed by a national opinion survey of 800 randomly selected respondents.

56   Richard Eckersley, *Quality of Life in Australia: An analysis of public perceptions*, Discussion Paper No. 23, The Australia Institute, Canberra, 1999, p. ix.

59   See Hamilton and Denniss, *Affluenza*, Chapter 9. The eight paragraphs commencing "Such a progressive politics" are taken in large part from this book.

63   Policies listed here are modified from the Wellbeing Manifesto. See <www.wellbeingmanifesto.net>.

65   On downshifting, see Clive Hamilton and Elizabeth Mail, *Downshifting in Australia: A sea-change in the pursuit of happiness*, Discussion Paper No. 50, The Australia Institute, Canberra, 2003.

65   "true autonomy": the distinction between individuality and autonomy is made well by Richard Eckersley. See, for example, "A Revolution in Wellbeing", a talk to the Communities in Control Conference, Melbourne, June 2004.

Hugh White

A *Quarterly Essay* provides space for a skilled essayist like John Birmingham to explore his topic from several angles. In *A Time for War* he makes the most of this opportunity, ranging from the hills of Afghanistan to the Bondi RSL. That journey becomes a kind of metaphor for the range of deeper questions he raises about the ways our attitudes to armed force, and to our armed forces, have evolved in recent years. The story moves from a glowing, almost hagiographic account of the exploits and qualities of Australian soldiers at Shahikot, via a meditation on Australia's idiosyncratic culture of military commemoration, to much darker questions about the nature of a new Australian militarism and the ways in which Australian governments have used our armed forces in recent years. Like many of us, Birmingham loves our warriors, but is much less sure about our wars.

All of this sets up tensions in the argument of the essay which are not fully resolved. That is not necessarily a fault. It means the essay itself becomes a demonstration of its key point: that our attitudes to military force are deeply ambivalent, and at times frankly contradictory. As Birmingham's quote from Kipling suggests ("*For it's Tommy this, an' Tommy that …*"), this is not new. Indeed a profound ambivalence to war, and warriors, is embedded in our culture, back to Homer.

That ambivalence has become more acute since about the start of the nineteenth century, with the rise of the Liberal Conscience. It was amplified in complex ways in the first half of the twentieth century, and then again more forcefully by the Vietnam War. After Vietnam, Western countries came to believe that, short of major war, there was very little that could be achieved by the use of armed force, and very few circumstances in which it was legitimate to try. And of course this was particularly true for the United States and Australia. Hence T.B. Millar's 1979 comment, quoted in the essay, that no one at that time was interested in deploying Australian forces overseas.

Since then, as Birmingham shows very well, the pendulum has swung back, and military operations are again seen by Western governments to be sensible and legitimate instruments of policy in a wide range of circumstances. The change started ten years before September 11, with the end of the Cold War, the (at first, timid) commitments to UN-sponsored peacekeeping operations, and especially the easy victory over Iraq in 1991. In Australia, as Birmingham says, the army's role in East Timor in 1999 took this trend to new heights. Armed force again became central to Australia's international posture, and the army regained its place as a central national institution. And the War on Terror has reinforced these trends — at least until Iraq.

But Iraq has clouded the picture a little. Some of the old ambivalence has returned. We have been reminded that we don't mind short, simple wars, but don't like ones that drag on and get complicated. We have been reminded again of some of the lessons of Vietnam — about how hard it is to achieve political objectives in foreign lands using military forces, for example, and how easily the job of fighting an insurgency can undermine one's own values and standards. And we have been reminded that, notwithstanding successes in East Timor and elsewhere, we still face some very tough questions about when and how it is wise and right to use our armed forces, and what kind of forces we should be building as a result.

Everyone can agree that weak and failing states pose serious long-term security problems. Everyone can agree that in some circumstances Western countries have both an interest and an obligation to intervene to help provide stability. Sometimes, military forces will be among the instruments we need to use. But there is a big step from these propositions to the idea that over coming decades the key role of Australia's armed forces will be — and should be — to undertake armed interventions in other countries in order to fix their internal problems. Shorn of persiflage, this is the idea which underlies much of the current discussion of Australian defence policy, and especially much current thinking about the future role of our army. And this is the idea that, with understandable ambivalence, Birmingham is wrestling with in his essay. It obviously worries him, but his admiration for the ADF is a counter-weight to those worries.

I do not share that ambivalence. I admire the ADF immensely, but I am very sceptical of the idea that armed forces can readily be applied to the tasks of stabilisation and nation-building. We have perhaps been seduced by the apparent success of operations like East Timor into thinking that the ADF, and especially the army, can do anything it is asked to do. The army, not surprisingly, encourages that view, and its self-publicity extols the effectiveness of soldiers in nation-building and diplomacy as well as combat. Individual soldiers may have such skills, but armed forces as institutions do not. An army is a highly specialised organisation designed, equipped and trained to perform a very specific type of task. That task is combat with other, similar armies.

Birmingham's doubts are assuaged by his belief that today's Australian Army is adapting to the new tasks of intervention and stabilisation through the publication of documents like the recent *The Australian Approach to Warfare*. I can't agree. The concept of manoeuvre which he says lies at the heart of that paper is all about conventional combat against an adversary's army. These are traditional concepts of continental land warfare, concepts that have much more to do with the world of Sir John Monash than with the world of T.E. Lawrence, or Osama Bin Laden. The army talks about new tasks, but is still preparing to fight old wars. Indeed the government's vision of a new hardened and networked army – buying tanks and amphibious assault capabilities – is taking the army closer to the heavy armies of the old Cold War, and further from the kind of light forces that stabilisation operations demand.

So while I think Birmingham has done a wonderful job of exploring the evolution of our attitudes to our armed forces, I am less confident than he is about the way ahead. I do not think that the army has now, or is evolving to acquire, the capacity reliably to achieve complex, non-military, essentially political objectives in a turbulent and unstable region. At best it can only make a partial contribution to those objectives; often it will have no role at all. So I think we should remain very conservative about the circumstances in which armed force is a good instrument of policy for other than conventional inter-state conflicts.

And we should not forget that, for Australia, situated where it is, the era of conventional inter-state conflict might be far from over. As Birmingham acknowledges, the challenge of terrorism is only one of a range of new security challenges: the rise of India and China are others. In coming decades Australia may well find itself living in a region torn by strategic competition, even conflict, among the great powers of Asia. If that happens, we will need all the military capability we can muster. But the forces we will need then are our naval and air forces. We are today the largest air and naval power south of China and east of India. That gives Australia real strategic weight. Our army, however hardened and networked, will always be the smallest serious army in Asia. The heroics of Shahikot notwithstanding, there are limits to what it can do for us if and when, in Kipling's phrase, "*the guns begin to shoot.*"

Hugh White

Michael Wesley

Reading *A Time for War* is a bit like watching the middle third of a movie. The reader is left to try to divine the origins of the events described, as well as their likely consequences. Although the essay is very thought-provoking, it is left to the audience to decide whether what Birmingham has discussed is significant and different, or whether rather too much has been made of these developments.

Birmingham lists several recent developments relating to Australia's armed forces – the increasing frequency of the ADF's deployment abroad, the emergence of a significant local defence industry, widespread public support for the armed forces and their ceremonies such as Anzac Day, the political kudos gained by both sides of politics for embracing the armed forces, the popular adulation of figures such as General Cosgrove – to imply that there's something noteworthy going on here. He flirts with two possible negative interpretations, both with a fascist tinge. At one stage he warns that "Liberal societies need to worry not when they are most divided, but when a paralysing homogeneity of thought takes hold," and uses the Iraq war as an example of how policy not debated leads to disaster. The implication at this stage seems to be that the mass adulation of the ADF may lead us away from our liberal ideals and towards foreign policy disaster. He doesn't mention that in Australia, as in the US and the UK, the Iraq war was preceded by extensive debate. John Howard scheduled three separate set-piece parliamentary debates on the Iraq war prior to invasion; these resulted not in the rational betterment of policy but in the government's masterful marginalisation of the Opposition and participation in a deeply flawed invasion strategy.

Next, Birmingham introduces the idea of a "new" Australian militarism, which, when fully developed, results in a society which has "adopted and exalted values traditionally favoured by military organisations, such as regimentation, aggressiveness, nationalism and the glorification of traditional structures ... [and gives] an increasing or predominant role to the military establishment in both national and international affairs". But then he backs away, suggesting that this moment is not yet upon us, as demonstrated by the difficulties the armed forces have experienced in finding recruits.

Birmingham's conclusion is a brighter one, reflecting the flashes of his own guilty exaltation of Australia's soldiers and their top-shelf gear. We are seeing "something more than a crude militarisation of Australian politics ... [or that] Australian governments will view every threat or problem through a militarised prism ... [or that] the Australian people have become more warlike or enthralled by military culture". Rather, "what it might all mean is that an adolescent, derivative culture is maturing ... it may be that Australians have come to a point at last where they feel confident not just of their place in the world but, more importantly, of their ability to act decisively in it."

Fair enough. But how did we get here, and where will this newfound confidence take us? In breathing a sigh of relief at signs of the "maturation" of Australia's "derivative and adolescent culture", Birmingham has to ignore the powerful external forces driving these developments, because one reading of these external forces would be that they demonstrate, once again, Australia's refraction of Western mindsets and values.

The quickening pace of ADF deployments abroad was less a response to domestic political factors than to a rapid rise in international demand for their use. The end of the Cold War and the first Gulf War saw Australia's strategic thinking remain firmly in lock-step with that of the United States and Europe: the new, post-containment name of the game was using multilateral coalitions to end civil wars and deter rogue states. More recently, deployments to Bougainville, East Timor and Solomon Islands have similarly followed Western strategic thought: at a time when our Atlantic allies were intervening against human rights abuses in the Balkans, so were we in East Timor; and when the agenda had moved to strengthening failed states, that became our mission in the Solomon Islands and Papua New Guinea.

There is also a simple explanation for the emergence of a local arms industry that doesn't rely on dark suspicions of a new militarism. As the world's thirteenth-largest economy, in an era of rising trade competition and close attention to countries' technological edge, it would be noteworthy if Australia hadn't bolstered its defence industries. As the difficulties of the Collins-class submarine showed, it would have been more cost-effective simply to buy off-the-shelf equipment. Nor does it mean that Australia doesn't source the vast bulk of its weapons from overseas.

Even the "end of Vietnam syndrome" proclaimed early on by Birmingham needs to be seen in the context of a parallel development in America, where the Republican ascendancy between 1981 and 1993 saw a conscious campaign to boost the legitimacy of the military, helped by a series of hammer-and-walnut interventions into Grenada, Panama and Kuwait.

Certainly, Australian forces have performed extremely well. Before Cosgrove, there was General Sanderson in Cambodia. While the US Rangers were being shot to pieces in Mogadishu, diggers were achieving miracles in Kismayu. It is natural that most Australians feel pride when their armed forces do well, just as they feel pride when their sporting teams do.

Looking for the sources of the seeming change in the ADF's role in Australian society raises questions about both the point of Birmingham's essay – that there is something significant happening here – and his tentative conclusion, that this represents a maturation of Australia's conception of its international role and capabilities. A key question here is, if the US retreats back into a second "Vietnam syndrome" after its misadventure in Iraq, while the ADF emerges without a casualty, will the tempo of ADF deployments abroad continue unabated? Or will Australia's military deployments again follow what America feels is necessary and achievable in upholding international order?

And if Birmingham is right, and we are indeed seeing a maturation of Australia's conception of its international role and capabilities, where will this take us in the vastly more complex world we are entering? As Australia's region sees the emergence of two great powers in India and China, neither Western nor allied to the West, each with a distinctive preference for regional order, to what purpose will its capacities and willingness to intervene be put? If the United States opposes a reshaping of regional norms, will this also become Australia's strategic mission?

Michael Wesley

Graeme Cheeseman

John Birmingham's *A Time for War* is revealing as well as interesting. His treatment of Australia's latest military adventure overseas – by elements of our Special Air Services (SAS) Regiment – evokes, consciously or otherwise, key elements of our military mythology. His SAS troopers are infused with the values and the spirit of the legendary Australian digger: iconoclasm, independence and gritty determination in the face of adversity. The story of the battle of Shahikot is nothing less than Gallipoli in Afghanistan. All that is missing are the (Australian) casualties and the consequent matting of Australian and American blood on a "Turkish" hillside. Australian citizens and military planners, it seems, are not the only ones having trouble escaping these particular "ghosts of battles past" – an underlying theme of Birmingham's essay.

He appears as well to be unduly trusting of, or receptive to, official pronouncements on Australian defence (or at least their military elements). The Defence Department's *The Australian Approach to Warfare* may accurately describe how our military forces have performed at the tactical level in conflicts past and present. Like all official policy prescriptions – and a good deal of Australia's military history – however, it (conveniently) ignores or downplays the overarching political and strategic contexts within which our armed forces practised and perfected manoeuvre warfare (to use its current moniker).

The most important contextual omission is the fact that, since Federation, Australia's military forces have been prepared for, and used primarily in, an imperial expeditionary role: as spear-carriers and shock troops for the various (anti-) colonising, homogenising and globalising projects of our imperial masters and benefactors. Michael Evans and others are right to suggest there is no place for strategy within such a schema. The basic role of our forces is the essentially symbolic one of flag-carrier. Evans et al. are wrong in at least one regard, though. Strategy and strategic doctrine remain important tools in providing a covering rationale for the forces and capabilities that are being developed to fulfil Australia's roles as loyal vassal and/or "deputy sheriff".

The need for strategic as well as political "spin" provides ample employment opportunities for our graduates in strategic and war studies (provided these days they also have a party-political pedigree). But it has a number of unintended consequences. One of these is the continuing (and ultimately irrelevant) discordance noted by Birmingham among what he calls Australia's strategic "policy wonks". Another is a degree of confusion on the part of planners at Russell Hill who, in line with the Defence Department's rationalist rhetoric, think Australia's military structures and capabilities should be derived logically from considered appraisals of our circumstances and interests. Still another, potentially more serious consequence is the inadequate preparation of our forces for their real rather than their publicly articulated roles. As Birmingham notes, this was revealed by Australia's East Timor experience. It was more evident still in Vietnam (for more on this see Greg Lockhart's forthcoming book *The Minefield*).

What is occurring today in Australian defence, then, is not altogether unusual or surprising. It reflects a trend that has continued more or less unbroken since at least the lead-up to the First World War (Labor's occasional genuflections to continental defence notwithstanding). It also need not have happened, but that is another story. As Birmingham argues, what is surprising in our latest bout of imperial militaristic fervour is the apparent lack of opposition and concern it is generating among Australians (unlike the situation in the United States). This, he continues, is unfortunate since public debate, criticism and dissent are crucial elements of a Western democratic tradition that serve to distinguish us from our totalitarian opponents. They also act as a key antidote to states and their leaders following "what Barbara Tuchman described as a march of folly – persistence in the face of reason". To underline his concern he contrasts the quietude of today's strategic commentary with the noisy radicalism of the 1980s and its prescient warnings about the emergence of a "new Australian militarism" – warnings he says that seem more apposite today than they did then.

The remainder of his essay looks at why there is an absence of critical debate on defence in Australia, as well as why we now appear to be pursuing new forms of militarism and patriotism. A third and related question of interest is what has led to the dramatic reversal in the public standing since Vietnam of Australia's armed forces. His answer to these important questions invokes three broad themes. The first is that mix of strategic-cultural forces – or primal fears and ambitions as Hugh White designates them – which serve to predispose Australians to particular ways of responding to the world around them. Long-schooled in the politics of fear and race (the latter not mentioned by either Birmingham or White), Australians have always tended to internalise (or "personalise") external threats and, conversely, to externalise their inner fears by projecting them onto such demonised (and racialised) "others" as Osama Bin Laden and Al Qaeda. Hence Australians have generally taken to heart the (largely exaggerated) assessments of the threat of international terrorism. They have broadly accepted the government's case for the country's participation in the American-led War on Terror. And they seem not to be worried about our (increasingly militarised) responses to an essentially non-military threat.

His second theme concerns the ongoing political, cultural and generational changes taking place within Australia itself. These see the transformation (or destruction) of the set of institutional arrangements and understandings – the "original Australian Settlement" to use Paul Kelly's phrase – that were established at Federation and provided the template for the Australian experiment. The anxieties and opportunities of this transformation, together with the uncertainties precipitated by the end of the Cold War and the acceleration of globalisation, are said to be leading growing numbers of young Australians in particular to seek succour and salvation in the old-fashioned yet powerful religions of evangelism and "diggerism" (Birmingham could well have added sport to his list). In a modern-day version of a familiar story, Australians are seeking to compensate for their anxieties by asserting a more confident, even strident form of nationalism and are looking more to their dead digger forebears than to their live baby-boomer parents for guidance in this quest. As a result they are flocking in ever-growing numbers to Anzac Cove and to the Australian War Memorial in Canberra. They are engaging in flag-waving and other patriotic displays that would have been unthinkable in the not-so-distant past. And, although critical of the war in Iraq, they have tended to support, or at least not criticise, our soldiers who are serving both there and in Afghanistan.

Key events and personalities can never, of course, be entirely excluded from such considerations, and so it is with Birmingham's analysis, which looks especially at John Howard, East Timor and Peter Cosgrove. The latter two are said to have been instrumental in the public renaissance of the Australian Defence Force (or the exorcism of the so-called "Vietnam syndrome" from the public consciousness). Howard plays a curiously muted role in Birmingham's story, as much a follower or victim of events as an active player. This sits rather oddly with the rest of his analysis. Taken together with his intermittent attacks on the "Left", we must wonder whether he has not succumbed to the growing tendency among public commentators not to be seen as a "Howard basher".

This last criticism aside, I think there is something in Birmingham's overall analysis, even though it is not altogether easy to follow. There are as well, however, important omissions and qualifications that need to be noted before drawing any final conclusions. Any appraisal of the contemporary defence debate in Australia has, for example, to take cognisance of the changing nature of policy-making in this country. As David Sullivan lamented in a 1996 essay, the post-Cold War period has witnessed the continued intrusion into academe of former members of the defence and security establishments. There they engage in a largely unreflective and non-critical strategic discourse, second-guessing their former departments and patrolling the intellectual borders of the Australian security debate. In some cases they are even commenting on policy prescriptions they themselves helped formulate. This process of politicisation and control has increased dramatically under the Howard government's tutelage and is a key reason for the paucity of critical strategic commentary in Australia today.

The experience of the 1980s tells us that this need not be so. The intellectual motivation for, and most of the energy behind, the publication of *The New Australian Militarism* came from the late Herb Feith, a tireless peace activist and internationally renowned scholar of Indonesian politics. Herb was determined that the Australian public should be made aware of the changes afoot under Labor's then defence minister, Kim Beazley. He formed the "Secure Australia Project", a group of academics, peace movement members, politicians and their political advisers. These discussed the issues, released public statements of concern on such matters as Australia's nascent defence industry and regional arms trade, and wrote two books. The first, published in 1990, was *The New Australian Militarism*. Its sequel, *Threats Without Enemies: Rethinking Australia's Security*, was published two years later. It was in many ways a more important (and prescient) work than its predecessor, arguing that Australia's principal sources of insecurity are now largely non-military in nature and must be dealt with co-operatively and empathetically. One of the greatest impediments to dealing successfully with these various "threats without enemies", it continued, was to allow the concept of security itself to remain overly militarised; exactly what has happened.

I have already criticised Birmingham for downplaying the Prime Minister's manipulation for political gain of the threat of terrorism. He has an obligation too, I think, to provide his readers with some sense of the politics that underpin his other key themes. As Graham Seal reminds us in his book *Inventing Anzac: The Digger and National Mythology*, our military myths and legends are largely invented traditions, constructed and maintained to serve particular political ends and interests. These included, after the First World War, the diversion of public attention away from the private losses incurred and onto the more ennobling (and less politically charged) notions of public duty and sacrifice; the absolution of our political and spiritual leaders from their part in the killing and maiming of their children and grandchildren; and the mobilisation of public sentiment against forces and ferments said to be threatening the stability and established order of post-war Australia. This was not, as Birmingham suggests, a process of strengthening Australia's foundations, but of using the power and the privileges available to the state to reinforce a particular social structure and its underlying value-preferences (a process that is being repeated, arguably, with the dismantling of the Australian settlement). I would suggest that the current debates fostered by John Howard and his foreign minister over Australian values and Australian history represent a continuation of this process, as does the Prime Minister's exploitation of fear and the flag to keep us in line and his government in power.

I am, however, at one with John Birmingham (and Barbara Tuchman among others) on the crucial role of public debate and (non-violent) dissent in the maturation and progress of societies (Western or otherwise). You might say that a baby boomer would believe that, even one who went through Duntroon with Peter Cosgrove and the rest of the Class of '68. I have confidence, though, that this sentiment is shared by a great many young as well as older Australians. The problem confronting us all is that the ideas needed for such debate don't exist in a vacuum. They are located in and need to be drawn from broadly based intellectual traditions as well as from a range of alternative narratives of, or perspectives on, our own history, culture, identity and changing place and role in the world. The predilection of this government in particular gradually to close down or restrict the opportunities and spaces for critical reflection raises genuine concerns about our capacity to grow beyond our present adolescent and largely derivative culture (to borrow Birmingham's words but not his conclusion). This is especially so given our innate anti-intellectualism, the continuing place of fear and anxiety in our imagination, and our continuing preparedness to obscure, repudiate, deny and expunge from our historical consciousness the more uncomfortable and politically unpalatable episodes of our past.

In military and strategic affairs especially we are, I believe, already engaged on a kind of "march of folly"; the legacy, I would suggest, of our First World War and earlier colonial experiences (that other story again). It has already led to the unnecessary death and suffering of thousands of innocent Australians. We have over time, it has to be said, got better at limiting the prospect of casualties. We continue, however, in the name of freedom, democracy and all the other epithets used by scoundrels, to place our young people and our future at risk. The stakes are high ones indeed, but well worth the cost and effort of continuing to speak out. Its limitations notwithstanding, John Birmingham's thoughtful essay achieves this last goal admirably.

Graeme Cheeseman

Rowan Cahill

Like John Birmingham, I am interested in the Australian way of war and "the renewed esteem of the military in our core culture". Unlike Birmingham, however, I do not draw comfort or satisfaction from this "reconnection", and cannot see it, as he does, as evidence of the maturation of an "adolescent, derivative culture". Nor am I surprised that there has "been surprisingly little sustained critique in Australia of what appears to be new and rapidly evolving doctrines such as pre-emption".

The re-emergence of the martial spirit in Australia is no accident of history. The "strange, contrary shift in both mass and elite opinion", the "reconnection" Birmingham writes about, is something that has been socially and politically engineered, from the mid-1970s onwards, by a coalition of interests intent on rebuilding Australia's armed forces after the demoralising lows and accumulated debilitating legacies of the Vietnam War era, including the domestic HMAS *Voyager* tragedy (1964).

Post-1972, Australia's armed forces, particularly the army, found themselves without an enemy, and with major problems regarding strategy, organisation, leadership, funding, morale, recruitment and equipment – all in a national cultural mood that was anti-war. The new, confident military mood that is the focus of Birmingham's essay is the end result of this rebuilding by politicians, defence personnel, lobbyists and an energetic international armaments industry, helped along the way by media-savvy defence interests, and by a legion of journalists, educators and historians who variously became part of the process. International terrorism, particularly in the wake of the 1978 Hilton bombing (Sydney), increasingly provided the enemy and rationale the Cold War no longer could, and the mythologising of Australia's military history overcame the antiwar legacies of the 1960s.

Birmingham touches on this mythologising process in his section "The

Ghosts of Battles Past", but I regard it as central to the new military mood in Australia. There is a dark complexity in the Australian cultural soul where Nation, Sacrifice and Blood mix, perhaps best expressed during the Boer War, years before Gallipoli and the Anzacs brought it all together, by the Australian poet who wrote:

> A nation is never a nation
> Worthy of pride or place
> Till the mothers have sent their firstborn
> To look death in the field in the face.

Before this, in 1885 when the colony of New South Wales sent a contingent of troops to support Britain during the Sudan crisis, the NSW politician H.S. Badgery expressed his hope that military involvement would act as a social cohesive, overcoming the colony's class and religious tensions, and "cement the people in this community of all classes and creeds in one common feeling".

Part of the "reconnection" process, as Birmingham acknowledges, is the "breathless idolatry that now accompanies every Anzac Day". Again, I suggest, this has not come out of the blue, but is part of the rebuilding process mentioned earlier. Just how it has happened, chapter and verse, awaits future historians, but involves politicians, the ADF, the RSL, veterans' organisations, the Department of Veterans' Affairs, the growing body of war historians, journalists, the travel industry (with a range of battle-site tours), among others, the end result being a general perception, one often expressed at Anzac Day commemorations by school student speakers, that "the freedoms" we have today are due to the sacrifices of Australians in wars past, and that the nation was forged at Gallipoli.

These are big calls, given that Australia's military involvements stretch from the land-grabbing participation in the Maori Wars during the 1860s (the troops were rewarded with grants of confiscated Maori land) to the present-day controversial involvements in Afghanistan and Iraq, with the only real threat to the nation coming during the Second World War. Sadly, the notion of the nation being forged by war sidelines and diminishes the long, complex, intricate, peaceful, creative process of nation-building that resulted in Federation in 1901.

The mythologising process distorts history, best seen in the passing of "The Last Anzac", Alec Campbell, in 2002 at the age of 103. Accorded a state funeral and eulogised by politicians and the media for his six-week career at Gallipoli as a sixteen-year-old soldier in 1916, there was little public acknowledgment that

Campbell had, for most of his adult life, thought war a futile activity and devoted much of his life to the trade union movement and the cause of peace. Indeed, so far as being "The Last Anzac" was concerned, he didn't even rate a mention in the book *The Last Anzacs* (1996), the mythologising process only catching up with him between 1996 and 2002 when he was, arguably, far from being in control of his own destiny.

The "religious tenor" of contemporary Anzac Day ceremonies noted by Birmingham should come as no surprise. Historian Dr John A. Moses, an ordained Anglican priest, has examined the theological roots of Anzac observance in "war theology", the idea among Australian clergy during the First World War that the British Empire had to be defended because the Empire provided the God-given opportunity to spread the Gospel into places it had not reached, that our troops were latter-day crusaders, that we were locked in a battle against anti-Christian forces; the first commemoration of the Gallipoli campaign was initiated by the churches (in Brisbane, 1915) and the first proceedings to establish Anzac Day as a commemorative event was dominated by the churches (in 1916), an aim being to establish a sacred day to "re-activate in all Australians, regardless of denomination, a sense of spiritual community under Almighty God".

Finally, a cautionary note. Despite Birmingham's sense of national maturation associated with Australia's new military prowess, I have reservations. There is a jingoistic tone about it all, flagged on the lapels of some of our leading politicians. In other cultures the manipulation of notions of Nation, Sacrifice and Blood has sometimes led to profound military misadventures abroad, even been a prelude to domestic authoritarian political practices. Here, I think, we need to be aware that the Australian martial tradition, aside from involvements overseas, also includes the use of the armed forces for domestic peace-time political purposes, a tradition stretching back to the strikes of the 1890s through to the breaking of the 1989 industrial campaign of the Australian Federation of Air Pilots. Recent changes to federal legislation under the justification of fighting the War on Terror potentially extend the basis upon which military force may legitimately be used against the civilian population.

Rowan Cahill

Correspondence

Bruce Haigh

I see John Howard as an incrementalist – he takes one or two steps forward and if unchallenged holds his ground; if challenged, he retreats but is ever ready to return. He is an assiduous acquirer of power.

Howard was fearful of getting militarily involved in East Timor. The strength of public opinion (until recently his only yardstick) pushed him into it. It was a success, and many political benefits flowed from it. Howard basked in the reflected glory. Hubris was his middle name.

He saw the benefit of being a khaki prime minister. September 11 and the rally to the so-called War on Terror reinforced the domestic political lessons learnt from East Timor.

Howard put together his own brew of Australian nationalism, which included easing the military toward the centre of the political stage through uses of the Anzac "tradition", military involvement overseas with significant media fanfare, support for the traditional sports particularly cricket and a condemnation of all activities and statements he decided were un-Australian.

The military was lauded for its role in border protection, even though many in the military were ashamed of it. The involvement in Afghanistan saved his bacon and that of the ADF, seen as it was as an honourable undertaking. Howard was among the first – if not *the* first – Western leader to commit to the US invasion of Iraq. His undertaking was given privately to George W. Bush just before mid-2002. The public announcement came eight months later.

Information about the activities and particular achievements of Australian troops has been kept under wraps in case of failure – another indicator of the increasing politicisation of the ADF under Howard. I understand the need to protect members of the ADF from being targeted by terrorists, particularly with respect to the SAS, but as with so many things under the Howard government, the balance has been lost. If the military undertaking is honourable and in

Australia's security interest, then a strong case can be made to keep the public fully informed as to what it is their young men and women have been tasked to do, and what they have achieved as a result. Howard is in the process of making the military into a secret organisation. The first step is hiding the identity of those involved in undertakings which the Australian public might not agree with.

The elevation of the military beyond critical examination or public scrutiny grew during the first ten years of the Howard prime ministership and no doubt will continue to grow. Little by little it is becoming, together with the AFP, his favourite and favoured arm of government.

The Auditor-General delivered a report on the Department of Defence at the end of 2005 which stated that over $750 million in defence assets was unaccounted for. No one in government (nor in opposition) seemed particularly concerned. The media had a brief look and moved on.

The ADF under Howard has achieved iconic status. It can carry out its activities without close scrutiny. Funding is not a problem. Together with the AFP, it enjoys the highest level of political protection. Its peace-time political status will be maintained, if not increased, provided it carries out the political agenda of government without question.

Cosgrove, the hero of East Timor, allowed the slide into Iraq without serious questions being asked. Robert Hill, like Alexander Downer, was a minister in name only. All major decisions relating to both departments are taken by the Prime Minister using the resources of his parliamentary office and the Department of Prime Minister and Cabinet.

The appointment of Brendan Nelson will change little. He was given the job to show that this government is serious about controlling defence spending, but it is not. As with border protection and refugee issues, funding is concomitant with whatever it takes. The Nelson appointment is all about spin. Ambitious as he is, Nelson is totally unprepared for the job. There is nothing in his background that might assist with decision-making. Headstrong and wilful, he might pause to consider that the position of defence minister has sunk quite a number of otherwise promising political careers.

It was Howard who pushed for the purchase of the Abrams tank (under pressure from the United States) and for the purchase, off the plans, of the US F35 all-purpose fighter. This decision ignored the history of the purchase of the F111, also off the plans. Cost blow-outs have already occurred. Howard (with Beazley's supine agreement) is likely to stick to the decision, but it will cost the Australian taxpayer an arm and a leg. And other options are available.

Why did Australian defence chiefs go along with this muddle-headed thinking? What is the pay-off? What are the fears and aspirations that allow them to suspend professional judgment?

As John Birmingham has indicated, the focus for future defence planning must be the region. The Abrams tank does not fit into regional scenarios and the F35 is overkill.

Howard has got the ADF into a position where he could use it to prop up falling or failing political support. Would he ever create an internal situation requiring deployment of the ADF or an Australian equivalent of Confrontasi? Would he attempt to shore up domestic support by an appeal to Australian nationalism and deployment of the ADF within the region in the hope of creating a repeat of the popularity following East Timor? Would he ever use the ADF to put down internal dissent or unrest? And would the ADF be prepared to be used in this way? Given the current political climate these are the questions that John Birmingham and other Howard watchers should be asking.

The ADF was used, if not abused, with "children overboard", the failure to act over *SIEV-X* and concealment of knowledge relating to prisoner abuse in Abu Ghraib prison in Iraq. The ADF has still not fully addressed, nor overcome, the issue of bullying. Many members feel they do not have adequate equipment to undertake assigned tasks. Recruitment levels consistently fall below requirement. All in all, despite Howard's hubris the ADF is not in good shape and further politicisation will benefit neither the ADF nor the Australian people.

Bruce Haigh

Paul Monk

Cartoonists delight in deriding the Prime Minister as "Little Johnny", but Johnny Birmingham's quaint notion of "taking off the gloves for a couple of rounds of bare-knuckled discourse" makes him a pretty good candidate for just that epithet. He makes plain, in his latest *Quarterly Essay*, that he regarded his rudimentary exchange with me after the publication of *Appeasing Jakarta*, four years ago, as exercise of the "bare-knuckled" kind. I find this really rather droll.

In that exchange, to the best of my recollection, I engaged in a bit of Marquis of Queensberry style sparring with Little Johnny, who responded by spitting, spluttering and waving his bare fists in the air to no discernible effect. But he'd made plain, before daring to get his "bare-knuckled" response to my remarks published, that he had lived a rather sheltered life. He insisted that I put in writing a commitment not to sue him for defamation, no matter what he wrote. That absurd nervousness showed, I suspect, how little taste he really has for vigorous verbal exchange.

That said, he seems to actually relish the idea of me girding my loins, greasing myself up and climbing into the cage in response to his latest essay, to borrow his curious phrasing. It doesn't seem to occur to him that, uninvited, I might have seen no point in commenting on his lucubrations. Leered at and challenged in such a manner, however, what sound gentleman could do other than put on his gloves once more to go the odd round with the silly mug? What harm can it do?

I think *A Time for War* is a better essay than *Appeasing Jakarta*. It is more temperate in tone, more judicious in many of its judgments and, in places, both interesting and even pleasant to read. Unfortunately, it otherwise suffers from many of the same faults as the earlier essay. It is a ramble through the subject, not a well-crafted argument. What seem, at least, to be its key claims, tend to pop up in the middle of discursive reflections, rather than as either the point of departure for, or the conclusion to, more systematic reflections.

Even more disconcerting is the author's tendency to arrive circuitously at a claim, then resile from it or contradict the grounds for it without giving any clear evidence that he realises what he is doing. I grant, of course, that he might be writing, more or less consciously, as a "postmodernist" of some kind, for whom such intellectual muddle is par for the course. As with other writing of that kind, however, this simply leaves the attentive reader puzzled as to what, at the end of the day, the author is actually trying to communicate.

At the clear risk of provoking another splenetic outburst of spluttering and fist-waving, I have to say that the way this essay is structured leaves the reader quite a bit of work to do to figure out whether its author had thought through his argument before writing it, or simply started writing and let such argument as came to mind emerge along the way. The essay begins with an untitled section highlighting the SAS's role in Afghanistan as a contrast with the Australian Army's role in Vietnam and indicating that a lot has changed, in recent years, in the Australian public's perception of the ADF. What it does not do is to state the author's central judgment – the point of the essay – and invite us to consider the case for it.

This would matter a little less if that central judgment was made somewhere and the case for it set out more or less lucidly. But it isn't clear that there is any such central judgment in the essay. Instead, what Birmingham does is wend his way backwards, by a long and winding road, through Afghanistan ("Ghosting the Desert" and "The Battle of Shahikot"), via a discursive rumination on "The Australian Way of War" and "Primal Fears, Primal Ambitions", to "Interfet and After" and then a reflection on "The Ghosts of Battles Past", which dwells on the legend of Anzac and the substantial revitalisation it has undergone in recent years.

Along the way, there are some nice passages, but the closest I could find to an argument that might be thought to hold the essay together is the idea that the ADF is, finally, becoming the defence force of a mature and self-respecting nation. If this is, indeed, Birmingham's view, he has come some way since his last Quarterly Essay. In that piece, he was all over the place as regards Australia's sense of itself, its economic prospects and its place in the region. He now appears to think that "since the election of Bob Hawke the Australian polity has by and large embraced a confident philosophy."

It is interesting that Birmingham should trace the growth in confidence to the Hawke government. He is pretty clearly reluctant to attribute it to the Howard government and appears to suggest, in his concluding remarks, that this growth in confidence has occurred and will continue despite the Howard ascendancy, not because of it. He states both that "the speed and efficiency with which the national economy has been transformed is remarkable" and that "despite the widespread fears of progressive thinkers that John Howard would like nothing more than to wind back the clock on forty years of social progress, it is indubitable that history cannot be wound back."

A few pages earlier, Birmingham had noted that, "while many, but not all, of Howard's social policies suggest a yearning for the days of Menzies, his economic philosophy is in no way conservative. It is all about dismantling the past." All this, I have to say, suggests that Birmingham still has quite a bit of thinking to do to straighten out where he stands. If the economy is powering ahead after almost a decade of John Howard's prime ministership, why write only of his desire to dismantle the past? Does Birmingham mean that dismantling the past is a prerequisite to economic transformation? If so, why not come out and say it? Credit where credit is due, Little Johnny.

More importantly, in terms of what seems to be his main line of argument, he implies, without ever stating it in as many words, that the transformation of the ADF somehow dates from the Hawke years. He no more pays tribute to John Howard and the Coalition here than he does in regard to economic policy. In reverentially and copiously quoting Hugh White, he sows further confusion in this regard. The transformation of the ADF has been the work of visionaries in the ADF who directly opposed Hugh White and his mentor Paul Dibb for years. It has been pushed hard by John Howard's government and in a direction clearly contrary to that imparted to it under the Hawke and Keating governments.

Had Birmingham been systematic in his thinking, he might have explored the ways in which the transformation of the economy was initiated by the Hawke and Keating governments, not out of confidence, as Keating made clear when treasurer, but out of alarm. There has been far more confidence over the past decade, as reform deepened and its fruits were harvested. What are the implications of this for the "progressive thinkers" Birmingham alludes to? – marginalisation as "tenured radicals" in many cases, their social agenda anchored in an economic philosophy being relegated to the famous dustbin of history.

He might, also, have explored the creation of the Defence of Australia (DOA) orthodoxy in the 1980s as a Labor compromise, caught between the Left's pathological antipathy to the maintenance of a serious military capability and the necessity to hedge against the possible failure of the ANZUS alliance to protect Australia's shores in extremis. He might then have examined more thoughtfully than he did the failure of the DOA to meet the country's actual security needs and the way in which the Coalition has tenaciously re-crafted strategic doctrine to meet the requirements of the early twenty-first century.

He does none of these things, even though he moves backwards and forwards across the terrain enough to show that, with a modicum of effort, he might have been able to do so. He quotes Michael Evans as having drawn on "the leading American strategic analyst Eliot Cohen to bolster his argument that the Defence of Australia doctrine has been effectively abandoned, even though, like Banquo's ghost, it just won't leave the table." Why not have gone the whole way with this colourful metaphor and aver that Hugh White is Banquo's ghost? Because he was too busy chatting to "Banquo's ghost" to take the full measure of what has transpired.

One gets the sense, taking Birmingham's two essays together, that he has been undergoing a slow transformation himself. It remains incomplete, though, and this is reflected in his still rather discombobulated way of making any kind of case. Thus it is that he finishes his most recent piece by writing:

> Just as the Australian economy has grown vast and become immeasurably stronger, so too has the old fearful, insular mono-cultural society passed away … It has taken more than two hundred years, but in finally confronting a world full of both threat and opportunity, it may be that Australians have come to a point at last where they feel confident not just of their place in the world but, more importantly, of their ability to act decisively in it. Whether that confidence is soundly based, however, is another matter.

This last, rather throwaway line exhibits Birmingham's own lack of confidence and uncertainty about how soundly based his claims are – nothing more. It is, surely, an odd coda to what immediately precedes it. Might he not have done better to have thought the matter through and offered us his judgment as to *whether* that confidence is soundly based? How much sense does it make to trumpet the idea that our economy has grown "vast" (compared with what?) and "immeasurably stronger" (than under Hawke and Keating?), that the old fears and shibboleths have been overcome, only to finish with a vacuous rhetorical question about whether the confidence derived from these things is "soundly based"?

I hope these few remarks will satisfy Little Johnny that I have taken note, at least, of his having poked his tongue out at me and bared his rear end like a good old-fashioned Gaelic clansman. I dare say he'll do some kind of hand-stand in response. What he'd be better served doing, though, is to stop making a spectacle of himself and concentrate, instead, on the Marquis of Queensberry rules of intellectual discourse – the rules of setting out a clearly structured argument and soliciting correction on key pieces of evidence and inference. When he does that, his essays will actually be worth more serious consideration. Oh, and he need have no fear that I'll sue him for defamation, whatever blue or purple prose he writes about me. Why would I bother?

Paul Monk

John Birmingham

Hugh White is too kind. He very kindly gave me a good deal of his time to answer my questions while I was researching *A Time for War*, and he has very kindly and gently dealt with the "tensions" and "ambivalence" he correctly discerns in the finished result. Like him I admire the men and women who have chosen the hard road of service in the Australian Defence Force. And like him I am wary of the ends to which they are sometimes put.

I don't know that there is actually much distance between us on the question of the army's suitability or preparedness for the sort of operations which fall outside its core business of war-fighting. I am with Cosgrove in believing it's easier for a traditional army to gear down to peacekeeping than it is for a police or paramilitary force to gear up for heavy combat. But I agree with White that the raison d'être of the army is to engage with an enemy and destroy it. Everything else is peripheral.

Does the Australian Army have a central role in the War on Terror? Probably not. It has a small but crucial role in theatres such as Afghanistan, but it's arguable that detectives and financial analysts from the AFP have played just as important a part in the wider effort, due to their role in attacking Jemaah Islamiyah. Diplomats, lawyers, forensic scientists, intelligence operatives and aid officials are among others making vital contributions.

In the end, quantity has a quality all of its own, and the Australian Army does not have a lot of mass to commit to the field against a serious opponent. I believe the government got a nasty shock when it realised this back in 1999, and even without September 11 we would have seen Canberra devote more resources to the ADF no matter which party was in office. The long-term strategic projections of Indian and Chinese power seem to leave policy-makers with few options. The rise of great powers is rarely a peaceful process. While the ADF is currently engaged in a number of nation-building and counter-insurgency operations, the force structure debate within the government seems to have been resolved in favour of equipping it for major combat operations within both urban and littoral environments. White is correct to point out that the army will bring less to these ventures than the navy and air force, which are both comparative heavyweights in regional terms.

It is a melancholy conclusion, but he is also right when he says that "the era of conventional interstate conflict might be far from over." Is it even possible to structure and fund a defence force that can safeguard national territory and interests from the traditional threats posed by rival nation-states, while simultaneously combating asymmetric threats from enemies such as Al Qaeda? The answer is a definite no at current levels of expenditure and staffing, but it might also be no at any level. Armoured regiments and long-range submarines are of no discernible use against a dirty bomb hidden in a rental truck. It doesn't mean they are in and of themselves useless, merely inappropriate for interdicting that particular class of threat. They remain entirely appropriate for responding to other classes of threat.

Whether such threats are real seems to be the point of Professor Wesley's reply, but he and I must be on very different wavelengths because I found myself having the same sort of problems with his reply as he seemed to have with the essay. Perhaps we were both free-associating a little too vigorously. Wesley appears to take issue with the idea that there has been any maturation of the Australian polity, leading to a conclusion, or perhaps just a speculation, that the seeming willingness of Australian governments to use force in pursuit of policy is nothing more than a reflection of American influence or, as he puts it, a "refraction of Western mindsets and values".

I do not feel overly confident reading too much into Wesley's comments, but it is almost as though he disapproved of the deployments to Bougainville, East Timor and the Solomon Islands, which he perceived to be of a sort with our "Atlantic allies … intervening against human rights abuses in the Balkans" and moving to strengthen "failed states" elsewhere. That may be unfair of me, however, and I may simply have mistaken his lofty academic detachment for a more censorious and judgmental intent.

On the other hand I am more than willing to take issue with him on the question of dissent. He imagines that because a very willing parliamentary debate failed to change government policy, such debate is pointless and devoid of true meaning, a proposition with which the early opponents of the Vietnam War would more than likely take issue. One debate in a chamber where the governing party not only had the numbers to enforce its will but also was more than happy to sink to any depths of mendacity and deceit in order to get its way is hardly reason enough to junk a tradition of two-and-a half thousand years' standing. The Iraq war is an unfolding story and may yet be years in the telling. Received wisdom and accepted truths of the day will be doubtless later thought of as grotesque lies and deception. So it's really rather immature of Wesley to sulk in a such a fashion when he could more profitably spend his time forensically examining the arguments made in favour of a war with which he disagrees. Nobody important may be listening yet, but the strength of an open political system lies in the fact that eventually they will.

Likewise it was somewhat disingenuous of the Prof. to play mind-reader and attribute some sort of *schadenfreude* to my "guilty exaltation of Australia's soldiers and their top-shelf gear". Sorry to disappoint, but there was no guilt there at all, buddy. Nor did I introduce the spectre of a "new Australian militarism". I simply wondered why such a concept, which received considerable attention in the 1980s, was dead in the water now.

As explained in the essay, it was Graeme Cheeseman and others who first coined the phrase, and it is Cheeseman who has provided one of the more interesting responses. I am worried, indeed alarmed, that he thinks I have been "unduly trusting of, or receptive to, official pronouncements on Australian defence". I specifically included the views of Cheeseman and iconoclasts such as Tony Kevin in an attempt to avoid such a pitfall. But it is possible he is correct, at least in part. I find his analysis of strategic doctrine as an important tool "in providing a covering rationale for the forces and capabilities that are being developed to fulfil Australia's roles as loyal vassal" to be as seductive as a siren song. It must be the old peace protester in me. It is also not a thousand miles removed from Murray Edelman's thesis of "politics as symbolic action", where outcomes and programs are less important than manufacturing consent among the governed. I'd be fascinated to see Cheeseman develop this idea further, to explain exactly how the process unfolds and how conscious the key players are of their roles in it. I have a wicked vision of the Australian Strategic Policy Institute's Aldo Borgu hunched over a keyboard rubbing his hands and cackling gleefully, "And now I shall do something really evil." But then I knew Aldo long before he worked for Peter Reith.

Otherwise I have no argument with Cheesemen's insights into the importance of such abstruse unquantifiable factors as race and fear. As he points out, I didn't mention them, but very easily could have. I'm probably less sanguine about the threat posed by Al Qaeda and its myriad franchises, but I don't doubt we both agree that the folly of recent adventures in Iraq has only added to the problem, while pushing Australia towards the top of the Islamists' target list.

Again, I'd hate to think that I have indeed "succumbed to the growing tendency among public commentators not to be seen as a 'Howard basher'". There are few things I enjoy more than a good tilt at the Rodent, but I do feel that many of my fellow travellers ascribe to him "Machiavellian superpowers" that he simply does not possess. I sat in the Liberal Party's campaign launch during the *Tampa* election, while covering it for the *Age*, and saw first-hand Howard's brutish exploitation of primal fears and his breathtakingly ham-fisted (and ultimately successful) co-opting of militarist imagery. So I have no illusions on that score. But as I pointed in the essay, Howard is scarcely unique in this way, and he is not even always successful. It's slightly off-topic, but I suspect that the electorate is gifting him with a very wide margin for ethical error. With so many voters living under a mountain of debt, and with the spectre (real or otherwise) of Islamist terror always hovering, I think the appeal of the traditional verities has been downgraded. Under such circumstances, people are entirely capable of thinking that the Prime Minister is a lying rodent, but not really caring very much about it, as long it doesn't affect them. In fact, it may even be considered an advantage under some circumstances.

If I have any regrets about *A Time For War*, it is simply that I wasn't able to contact Cheeseman to interview him before going to print. He makes a number of excellent points here which I would have been more than happy to pinch for myself.

I don't know that I can get as far out on the curve as Bruce Haigh when he foresees a short jump from the SAS to a domestic SS under John Howard, but I can only agree with him that the Howard government's obsession with secrecy surrounding the ADF is becoming counter-productive. Operational security is one thing. Image and issue management is entirely another. I am one of those who will always believe that the *Tampa* was a political circus, not a national security crisis calling for the application of military force. It was only via the Orwellian control of information flowing from the *Tampa* that Reith and Howard were able to maintain the election-winning fiction of "children overboard". Their shameless abuse of both the ADF and the asylum seekers caused great tensions within the services, particularly the navy, which did nothing to improve the functioning of the nation's military.

Like Cheeseman, Rowan Cahill would have preferred a longer, more forensic consideration of the forces behind the increased idolisation of Australia's martial tradition and especially the mythologising of Anzac Day. Having read his views on this now, I can only agree. We probably part ways on the small stuff. I would agree with him that the Second World War was the only clear and immediate threat to Australia's national existence, but I doubt he would agree with me that a German victory in the Great War would have seen a very different, and much darker, history of the last century. Nor do I imagine he would pay much heed to the argument, which I find compelling, that communism needed to be contained and eventually strangled to death for the good of humanity. However, his point about the mythological power of martial imagery and history is well taken and I should have extended my analysis in that direction, having started the process by examining the role of primal fears and the exploitation of those fears.

Finally, a great truism of showbiz is that in order to keep the audience waiting for more, one should leave the best till last. Unfortunately, all I have is Paul Monk, or as he shall now forever be known to aficionados of these marvellous correspondence pages, the Monkey.

Where to start?

A little history, perhaps. The replies to my previous *Quarterly Essay*, *Appeasing Jakarta*, were for the most part critical, but considered. However, one stood out for the intemperateness of its tone, the pompous gittishness of its author, and the remarkably swift descent from impersonal discourse to personal abuse. I think we all know who we're talking about.

Having replied formally to the other correspondents, I'm afraid I found myself at a complete loss when contemplating the Monkey's inexplicable nastiness. However, it's always been my belief that when someone decides to give you a poke in the eye, you give them one back, with maybe a kicking or two thrown in for good measure. So my reply to him was in kind; vicious, insulting, one-eyed and defamatory. It was a two-way street. And enormous fun into the bargain.

We did indeed have an agreement not to sue each other, precisely because the Monkey struck me as the sort of thin-skinned, self-important little meat puppet who would be only too happy to hand out the rough stuff, but would squeal when he got some back. Given the high-pitched screeching and genital grabbing in which he indulges himself here, I feel confident that most people would agree it was only prudent. And it has provided a wonderfully unexpected comedic windfall in the form of the Monkey's delusional self-portrait of an Indiana Jones-like adventurer on the wild, outer limits of public discourse. An image, I'm afraid, that contrasts strikingly with my understanding that when he received the response to his original note, he was left speechless and shaking. But of course, I wasn't there in person to witness it, so I couldn't possibly comment.

What I can comment on is his latest foray into the big boy's playground. Frankly, I find it hard to believe he's gone back there again. I thought we'd dealt with his inability to follow any line of argument or narrative that didn't proceed along the simple, one-track progression of a kindergarten storybook last time, but perhaps during his own, doubtless extended, stay in kindy he didn't receive a properly balanced diet and it has somehow stunted his brain. This would explain why the Monkey is so puzzled by arguments that everyone else seems to have had no trouble following, even if they disagreed with them. It's an achingly poignant scene, don't you think? The poor wee devil stuck at the back of the class, tears in his eyes because he still can't unravel the secrets of *The Cat in The Hat* while all other kiddies have proceeded on to Harry Potter or Narnia.

This incomprehension leads him down some remarkable paths. Whereas Cheeseman and Cahill were unsettled by a positive and apparently unquestioning view of the Howard government, for the Monkey the essay reads like standard-issue boilerplate from the op-ed pages of *Green Left Weekly*. Likewise he was left scratching his noggin and wondering why one of the main lines of argument, that "the transformation of the ADF somehow dates from the Hawke years", is never actually stated in so many words, when in fact that very point is stated over the course of thousands of words in the section on Beazley's time as defence minister and the resulting debate over the "New Australian Militarism".

As to all of his other problems, well, they really are his problems, not mine. And they are legion.

John Birmingham

John Birmingham's books include *Leviathan*, a history of Sydney, *He Died with a Felafel in His Hand*, *Dopeland* and the *Weapons of Choice* series. His essay *Appeasing Jakarta* was the second in the *Quarterly Essay* series.

Rowan Cahill is a labour movement historian and journalist. He was a conscientious objector during the Vietnam War.

Graeme Cheeseman is co-editor of *The New Australian Militarism* (1990), *Discourses of Danger and Dread Frontiers: Australian Defence and Security Thinking after the Cold War* (1996) and *Forces for Good? Cosmopolitan Militaries in the 21st Century* (2004). He is a former army officer, university lecturer and member of the Secure Australia Project.

Bruce Haigh was a diplomat from 1972 to 1994, during which his postings included Pakistan, Afghanistan, South Africa, Saudi Arabia and Iran. From 1995 to 2000 he was a member of the Refugee Review Tribunal. He served with the Royal Armoured Corps from 1966 and 1967. He is the author of two books, *The Great Australian Blight*, on Australia–Indonesia relations, and *Pillars of Fear*, on regional defence issues.

Clive Hamilton's book *Growth Fetish* was published in 2003, and his most recent book is *Affluenza*, co-authored with Richard Denniss. Hamilton is executive director of the Australia Institute, an independent think-tank based at the Australian National University. He is a former academic economist and senior public servant.

Paul Monk is the author of *Thunder From the Silent Zone: Rethinking China* (2005) and *Sonnets to a Promiscuous Beauty: A Homage to the Western Canon* (2006). His essays on geopolitical and cultural affairs appear regularly in the *Australian Financial Review*.

Michael Wesley is Professor of International Relations at Griffith University and Director of the Asia Institute there. He is the author, with Allan Gyngell, of *Making Australian Foreign Policy*.

Hugh White is a Visiting Fellow at the Lowy Institute and Professor of Strategic Studies at the Australian National University.

www.ingramcontent.com/pod-product-compliance
Lightning Source LLC
Chambersburg PA
CBHW081403270326
41930CB00015B/3395